T0324537

# Childhood
# in African Literature

Editor:           Eldred Durosimi Jones, Fourah Bay College,
                  University of Sierra Leone, Private Mail Bag,
                  Freetown, Sierra Leone.

Assistant Editor:  Marjorie Jones

Associate Editors:  Simon Gikandi
                   Department of English Language & Literature,
                   University of Michigan 7609 Haven Hall,
                   Ann Arbor, MI. 48109-1045, USA

                   Nnadozie Inyama
                   Department of English, University of Nigeria,
                   Nsukka, Nigeria

                   Francis Imbuga
                   Literature Department, Kenyatta University,
                   PO Box 43844, Nairobi, Kenya

                   Emmanuel Ngara
                   Office of the Deputy Vice-Chancellor,
                   University of Natal
                   Private Bag X10, Dalbridge 4014, South Africa

                   Ato Quayson
                   Pembroke College, Cambridge CB2 1RF, UK

Reviews Editor:    James Gibbs, 8 Victoria Square, Bristol BS8 4ET, UK

[The reviews section is restored in this issue.
Publishers wishing to submit books for review
should send them direct to the Reviews Editor.]

# Childhood
# in African Literature

*A review*

*Editor:*  Eldred Durosimi Jones

*Assistant Editor:*  Marjorie Jones

*Associate Editors:*  Simon Gikandi
Nnadozie Inyama
Francis Imbuga
Emmanuel Ngara
Ato Quayson

*Reviews Editor:*  James Gibbs

JAMES CURREY
OXFORD

AFRICA WORLD PRESS
TRENTON N.J.

James Currey
an imprint of Boydell and Brewer Ltd,
PO Box 9, Woodbridge, Suffolk IP12 3DF, UK
and 668 Mount Hope Avenue, Rochester NY 14620-2731, USA
www.jamescurrey.com
www.boydell and brewer.com

Africa World Press, Inc.
PO Box 1892
Trenton
NJ 08607

A catalogue record is available from the British Library

ISBN 978–0–85255–521–7

Transferred to digital printing

# Contents

**Editorial Article**
Childhood Before & After Birth

Eldred D. Jones

The pre-existence of unborn children in a fore-world is a widely held belief in Africa. Hopeful mothers sit under particular trees to woo the spirits of these children, many of whom consent to be born and survive the traumas and the uncertainties of childhood. Others, however, are reluctant to leave their paradisial environment and after a short troublesome childhood plague their mothers by returning to their spirit companions in the other world. These children, *abiku* among the Yoruba, *ogbanje* among the Igbo, made an early appearance in modern African literature in the twin Abiku poems of J. P. Clark and Wole Soyinka. Clark's poem, written from the point of view of the distressed mother, woos the child to stay:

> Then step in, step in and stay
> For her body is tired,
> Tired, her milk going sour
> Where many more mouths gladden the heart.[1]

Soyinka's child by contrast is wilful and mischievous, scorning the tears, the sacrifices and the amulets of the plagued mother:

> Must I weep for goats and cowries
> For palm oil and the sprinkled ash?
>
> Mothers! I'll be the
> Suppliant snake coiled on the doorstep
> Yours the killing cry. (*MPA*, p. 152)

Achebe's Enzima, the precocious daughter of Okonkwo, the only female for whom this stern unbending father seemed to have any respect and tenderness, similarly ('she should have been a boy') plagued her parents with her constant illness in childhood resulting from her being an *ogbanje*.

Soyinka's childhood companion, Bukola, an extended portrayal of a real life *abiku*, bragged of her ability to keep in touch with her spirit companions and mischievously used her status to blackmail her

1

anxious parents whenever they withheld anything she wanted. Although separated by many years the early poem carries items of vocabulary which recur in the later autobiography *Aké*. The fictional type in the poem had been 'earthed' with amulets: 'Yams do not sprout in amulets/To earth Abiku's limbs' (*MPA*, p. 152). Bukola was similarly 'earthed': 'Amulets, bangles, tiny rattles and dark copper-twist/rings earthed her through ankles, fingers, waist. She/knew she was *abiku*.'[2]

Though a mere child, Bukola had a tyrannical hold over her parents because of her powerful duality. She demanded feasts, *saara*, and when on one occasion her harassed father, the mission bookseller, baulked at yet another feast, the wilful child threw one of her spectacular faints and the old man had to produce an extra fowl for the inevitable feast to placate Bukola's spirit companions. Bukola was no doubt the inspiration for the portrait of the *abiku* child in Soyinka's poem.

Ben Okri includes a reference to Wole Soyinka in his acknowledgements in his epic novel *The Famished Road*. The title is an even more significant pointer to Soyinka's influence for it derives from a line in the poet's 'Death in the Dawn': 'And the mother prayed, Child/May you never walk/When the road waits, famished' (*MPA*, p. 146). Azaro, the *abiku* child narrator of Okri's remarkable novel (and its sequel, *Songs of Enchantment*) is a pilgrim on the carnivorous road, one of the most persistent symbols in the two novels. On more than one occasion, he is pictured inside the belly of the road – 'You are in the under-road' ... 'The stomach of the road'[3] – which swallows men as well as the forests and its inhabitants on its relentless progress to nowhere in particular:

> The road swallows people and sometimes at night you can hear them calling for help, begging to be freed from inside its stomach. (*FR*, p. 121)

Azaro himself is a victim of this devouring monster as he travels simultaneously through this and other worlds.

In a densely symbolic novel, Okri creates the whole imaginative Yoruba cosmos consisting of life before birth and a world in which ordinary human beings co-exist with spirits, devils and monsters, all of whose lives merge and influence one another. Not the least of his creations is his world of the unborn children in the lyrical opening of the first of the two novels. The world which the real-life Bukola sees only indistinctly (to her friend Soyinka's question 'Do you remember anything of the other world?' she replies 'No') (*Aké*, p. 16), is here portrayed as a paradise which children are reluctant to leave for the hazards of the real world:

> In that land of beginnings spirits mingled with the unborn. We could assume numerous forms. Many of us were birds. We knew no boundaries. There was much feasting, playing, and sorrowing. (*FR*, p. 3)

The 'sorrowing' was caused by the tales of disillusionment that their returning companions had brought from the world of the living, with the result that 'there was not one amongst us who looked forward to being born' (*FR*, p. 3). Untypically, Okri's Azaro elects to stay in the earthly world resisting blandishments and sometimes murderous attempts on his life by his spirit companions who wanted him back in their fore-world. Azaro is by this made into a much more positive character, a willing pilgrim prepared to share the adversities of poverty, political exploitation and general misery of his parents and others of their class. Ade, the other *abiku* introduced late in *The Famished Road* is more typical of the reluctant *abiku* child, world weary, always longing to return to his spirit companions (*FR*, p. 487).

Azaro moves in this mundane world simultaneously with a heightened existence which keeps him in contact with the spirit world and which enables him to 'see' all the fantastic spirits which populate the Yoruba paranormal cosmos. He is both a real child and a symbol of a nation in turmoil, indeed the nation itself is an *abiku*. 'Our country is an *abiku* country. Like the spirit-child, it keeps coming and going' (*FR*, p. 478).

By adopting the device of making his child narrator an *abiku* with this extraordinary gift of second sight which puts him in a superior position to his parents and other normal people, Okri eliminates the necessity to explain Azaro's extraordinary powers. It is therefore unnecessary for the author very late in the development of Azaro's story – indeed in the second novel – to attempt any kind of explanation for his ability as a little boy scarcely out of infant school being able to read everything from current journalism to ancient philosophy. His reservoir of all branches of knowledge had been poured into him by his spirit-companions.[4] Azaro is doubly alienated; an exile from the spirit world, he is also isolated from the ordinary world because of his familiarity with the paranormal. He is the victim of both. At the most elementary level of the dual existence he is cuffed by his anxious, uncomprehending mother when she finds him in conversation with his spirit-companions who are trying to seduce him back (*FR*, pp. 7–8).

Azaro moves in these two worlds, suffering with the world of men and contending with the consequences of his superior knowledge. He is a victim with the rest of the Nigerian world but he suffers at an even more intense level because he can even hear the groans of the forest trees as they fall bleeding under the mindless crunching of the bulldozer. He can see them bleed, he feels the devastation of the land with an intensity denied to ordinary mortals. Azaro thus moves through the novel burdened by the weight of the world on his young shoulders. He is an extraordinary choice for the narrator of a novel which is to portray the physical and spiritual degeneration of a nation informed by the whole wealth of human knowledge.

It is through Azaro's eyes that we see the whole corrupt society: the
exploitation of the masses, the growth of a heartless capitalism, the
corrupting influence of dishonest politics, the increasing poverty of
ordinary people. The boy sees Madame Koto, one of the main symbols
of this degenerating society develop from a normal roadside bar keeper,
a motherly neighbour, into an obscene bloated embodiment of the
corrupt society, and it is the little boy who carries the weight of Madame
Koto's malevolent influence:

> All around in the darkness Madame Koto was growing. She was growing in
> our room. Her great invisible form surrounded us in the dark, filling out the
> spaces . . . Her body encompassed us and wherever we tried to go her shadow
> was there . . . (*SE*, p. 42)

The narrative style often makes no concession to the natural expectations from a boy who is hardly out of infant school, as it measures up
to the extraordinary visions that Azaro sees, any one of which would
have deranged an ordinary little boy:

> All around me were silent figures in great masks. All around me were
> ancestral statues. Wherever I rode I saw immemorial monoliths with solemn
> faces and beaded lapis lazuli eyes. The monoliths were of gold, self-
> luminating in the darkness. One of the statues moved and turned into
> Madame Koto. Her golden wrapper fluttering about her, she climbed on to a
> caparisoned horse of the night and commanded the other statues and
> monoliths to follow her. (*FR*, p. 139)

These are hardly the vocabulary items of a boy of Azaro's natural age,
but at other times he is the little boy trying to come to grips with his
own mysterious capabilities and the mysteries that they enabled him to
see. It is a child who ruefully reflects 'That was the first time I realised it
wasn't just humans who came to the marketplaces of the world. Spirits
and other beings come there too' (*FR*, p. 16). The author's prose varies
with the demands of the particular occasion. Watching the agony of his
father accumulating suicidal loads in an attempt to make the maximum
amount of money in the shortest possible time, Azaro adopts an
appropriate syntactically cumulative style:

> He went on staggering, balancing the weights, slipping and miraculously
> regaining his footage, grunting and sweating, uttering the words 'MORE!
> MORE!' under his breath, and when he went past me I noticed that his
> crossed eyes were almost normal under the crush, and his muscles trembled
> uncontrollably, and he groaned so deeply, and he gave off such an unearthly
> smell of sweat and oppression that I suddenly burst into tears. (*FR*, p. 146)

There are the grand sweeps of language as when the little boy sees
through time and things in one of his visionary adventures:

> I saw [the converging spirits of the continent] in their transfigured procession
> . . . bringing their spirit-mysteries, their oceanic wisdom, their gnomic lore

distilled from countless incarnations, bringing the jewelled terror of their immanent foresight, and their understanding of the secret forces and balances in the universe. (*SE*, pp. 40–41)

Because of the towering stance, the cosmic vision with which the novels endow Azaro, the normal relationship between parents and child is reversed. As the whole narration nears its end in the *Songs of Enchantment* however, when the father has come out of his cleansing experiences, he resumes something of his parental authority and the boy becomes a boy again. It is the father who is the source of wisdom through experience of the earthly world:

He paused, breathed deeply, put his arm round my neck, fondled my hair, lifted his head to the sky, and said, in a voice quivering with mystery: 'But, my son, I think we have the WHOLE UNIVERSE inside us when we are joyful and full of life.' (*SE*, p. 133)

In the real world in spite of Azaro's *abiku* status, in spite of his access to the spirit world, the authority of the father is restored. If the *abiku* child is to remain in the world he is subject to this authority and to the conditions in which this authority prevails. The family remains as it had begun, the victims of oppression and dire poverty. Azaro has to bear these conditions as the consequence of his choice to remain in the world.

It is no diminution of Ben Okri's extraordinary achievement in *The Famished Road* and *Songs of Enchantment* to see parallels with Wole Soyinka's childhood reminiscences in *Aké*. Okri's work is still different and original. Like the real life autobiography, Okri's fictional narration employs the first person narrative style. The young Soyinka, another Yoruba boy, sensitive and precocious, had slowly discovered his environment, first within the protected compound of the parsonage: the headmaster's house (his father's), St Peter's Church, the school, the numinous presence of a dead bishop and the bushes in which lurked creatures of the traditional Yoruba forest. Even here, echoes of the mysterious Yoruba cosmos penetrated as in Wild Christian's (Soyinka's mother) childhood reminiscence of a family encounter with an *iwin* which had chased them back home from a snail-gathering expedition. This was no fantasy:

. . . It was only this figure of fire that I saw and he was still very distant. Yet I heard him distinctly, as if he had many mouths which were pressed against my ears. Every moment, the fireball loomed larger and larger. (*Aké*, p. 7)

Brother Sanya, the leader, in this episode was himself an *oro* 'which made him at home in the woods, even at night' (*Aké*, p. 5). The invasion of the *iwin* into the Christian household was sternly terminated by the Rev. J. J. with his hand on his Bible (*Aké*, p. 7). Even at school there were similar echoes from the other world. Osiki, one of Soyinka's playmates, actually had 'an *egungun* which emerged from their compound every year' (*Aké*, p. 31). This cohabitation between men, ghosts, forest creatures and ancestral spirits was part of the 'ordinary' Yoruba world. The traditional influences which only faintly penetrated the parsonage at Aké were even more apparent in Isara, the realm of Soyinka's grandfather who protected his grandson from potential enemies in dark ceremonies kept secret from his pious Christian mother.

The child Soyinka significantly widened his world when climbing over the parsonage wall he literally took to the road in the wake of the police band and for the first time encountered the world outside. Almost everything he saw was a source of wonder. Like Okri's Azaro, he was fascinated by the market and its varied wares and market women (both mothers, Soyinka's and Azaro's were market women) but even ordinary stalls had their own special thrill: 'And SALT! Nobody surely, not even the whole of Aké could eat so much salt in a hundred years' (*Aké*, p. 41). But Soyinka's market remained peopled with ordinary mortals and the most frightening sight was that of the withered old women who sat behind their weird displays of 'shrunken heads' from whom he fled in terror. Azaro's marketplace was a much more unearthly place scaling upwards from ordinary wares and ordinary people to 'people who walked backwards, a dwarf who got about on two fingers, men upside-down with baskets of fish on their feet . . .' (*FR*, p. 15). Soyinka endowed ordinary things with the wonder of discovery while Okri luxuriated in the more bizarre areas of the Yoruba imagination. It was the adult Soyinka who recollected his childhood in his maturity and whose prose heightened the commentary. Similarly in *The Famished Road* and *Songs of Enchantment*, while the hands were the hands of Azaro the voice was most certainly that of Okri.

Christopher Okigbo's death in the prime of his poetic powers is one of the great tragic stories of modern African literature. He embraced both the cause of Biafra and his death in one passionate gesture running to his premature end with a willingness verging on longing. Okigbo's life and his poetry formed one indissoluble unity; the poetry was his life. His own testimony makes explicit elements which are only suggested in the poetry and have to be searched for, a poetry which arose from a quest for self-discovery: 'And when I talk of looking inward to myself, I mean turning inward to examine myselves.'[5] The use of the plural 'myselves' signifies not only the horizontal influences that make up his poetic personality, birth, education from the nonsense approximations to the sounds of English nursery rhymes, his later exposure to classical and other civilizations through many life experiences including the near death of total anaesthesia; but also his vertical origins, his ancestry and its traditional paraphernalia. He was believed to be, and he believed himself to be, the incarnation of his grandfather, the priest of Idoto and it was his recognition of his failure to succeed his grandfather in the priesthood that brought him naked as a penitent to Mother Idoto's shrine in the opening lines of 'Heavensgate'.

This belief in incarnation is a significant informing element in his poetry and it is not surprising to discover, for example, with Catherine Acholonu in her article, 'Ogbanje: A Motif and a Theme in the Poetry of Christopher Okigbo',[6] that the myth of the *ogbanje* is a persistent recurring image in the poetry, a persistent self-image. Inherent in the idea of *ogbanje* is that of early death or rather return and Okigbo frequently foreshadowed his own early death.

Hitherto, in treatments of the death of an *ogbanje/abiku*, it is the sense of loss that has been highlighted; but the notion goes further and the cycle is a continuing one of birth, return and rebirth. Okigbo seems to have been very conscious of the more positive component of the cycle, that of reincarnation. His belief in incarnation as his poetry seems to suggest, is the one mitigating consolation for his untimely *ogbanje* departure. For the end is not really the end and the poetry sometimes shines with the brightness of hope of a future return:

> AN OLD STAR departs, leaves us here on the shore
> Gazing heavenward for a new star approaching;
> The new star appears, foreshadows its going
> Before a going and coming that goes on forever[7]

African authors have consistently returned to childhood to find their personal as well as their racial roots. Far from being merely nostalgic yearnings for a lost paradise, many of the treatments of childhood have exposed a grim reality of cruelty, harshness, parental (particularly paternal) egocentricism and extraordinary bruisings of the vulnerable child psyche. Yvonne Vera, for example, in her novel *Under the Tongue*, has treated one of the cruellest features of childhood anywhere, that of child rape, an abuse which is studiously covered by a cult of silence which this novel boldly shatters. The child, Zhizha, wakes up to find herself violated by her own father but her tongue is weighted down by this cult of silence:

> I feel my eyelids fall while my tongue grows thick and heavy, pressed between my teeth. My tongue is hard like stone. I dare not cry or breathe.[8]

This novel stands as a sterling example of the social responsibility of African authors in their portrayals of childhood.

---

## NOTES

1. Gerald Moore & Ulli Beier, eds, *Modern Poetry from Africa* (London: Penguin, 1970): 117.

2. Wole Soyinka, *Aké* (London: Rex Collings, 1981): 16.
3. Ben Okri, *The Famished Road* (London: Vintage, 1991): 17.
4. Ben Okri, *Songs of Enchantment* (London: Vintage, 1993): 5.
5. Marjory Whitelaw, 'Interview with Christopher Okigbo, 1965,' *The Journal of Commonwealth Literature*, July 1970:36.
6. Catherine Achonolu, 'Ogbanje: and a theme in the poetry of Christopher Okigbo' in *African Literature Today* 16 (London: James Currey and Trenton: Africa World Press 1988): 103.
7. Christopher Okigbo, 'Path of Thunder' in *Labyrinths* (London: Heinemann, 1971): 72.
8. Yvonne Vera, *Under the Tongue* (Harare: Baobab Books, 1996): 106.

# Carving a Niche: Visions of Gendered Childhood in Buchi Emecheta's *The Bride Price* & Tsitsi Dangarembga's *Nervous Conditions*

## Pauline Ada Uwakweh

This paper argues that biological identity notwithstanding, gender identity is constructed through the socialization of a child. It also posits that the *Bildungsroman* or the novel of development exemplifies gender identity in the making. Starting from birth, through childhood to adulthood, social expectations for the male and female child differ and grow in ever-widening circles, reaching a stage where each child inculcates the roles of their kind. As Buchi Emecheta's *The Bride Price* (1976) and Tsitsi Dangarembga's *Nervous Conditions* (1988) depict, breaking out of gendered roles or expectations is fraught with social and psychological conflict especially for women who must transcend gender expectations on the road toward independence.

### The gender factor in the African literary terrain

Gender identity, and its exclusionary potentials for the female are deeply rooted in the fabric of traditional and modern African societies. Gender determines women's status, roles in the domestic/private spheres and the levels of their participation in the political/public spheres.

The late development of an African female literary tradition has roots in the gender factor. Compared to the male tradition, the female tradition in African literature is a recent phenomenon. This historical circumstance is attributable to the fact that, 'women did not enjoy comparable educational opportunities, so that correspondingly fewer acquired the literacy, let alone the university education, that have traditionally been prerequisites for the writing of African literature in European languages' (Brown, 1981, p. 4). Gender politics permeates all aspects of African social life. Thus, it is no historical accident that most African *Bildungsroman* prior to the 1970s were written by men. Consequent upon colonial reinforcement of gender dichotomy, the African male became the privileged inheritor of formal European education.[1] The female was disadvantaged by the fact of her gender, her role confined to domesticity, and excluded from more lofty pursuits such as education. However, since the 1970s, the surge of literary writings by women is redressing the imbalance created primarily by the gender factor as well as colonialism in traditional African societies.[2] Even in the modern context of African societies, the effects of these two forces continue to haunt women. There is urgent need, therefore, for more attention to the ramifications of gender identity and its implications for the African woman. Africanists and gender theorists alike emphasize the need for a balance, a revision, or the establishment of egalitarian national governments that incorporate gender-planning in their public policy matters affecting women.[3] Ironically, literary critics are yet to address definitively the gender issue in literature.[4]

Notably, the African female *Bildungsroman*, is an exposé of gender construction in patriarchy, where maleness is socially esteemed and femaleness valued only as an ideal of continuity. It is, therefore, an illustrative resource on female development. Childhood for girls is dotted with silent frustrations that sometimes translate to self-defining actions; actions that may be expressed in revolt and are intended to transcend social limitations.

Central to the *Bildungsroman* tradition is the quest for education. Interestingly, male and female writers alike approach this issue from uniquely different perspectives. From male writers' perspectives, the hero, usually male, his world unfolding before him, is the focal point of exploration. His female counterparts (sisters, mothers) are oftentimes tangential to his heroic pursuits. They form the backdrop; their limitations contrasting markedly with the ebullient ambition exhibited by the male hero. While he strives for achievement in the public sphere, educationally or politically, the women remain in the private sphere, confined by tradition and gender to limited roles. Camara Laye's *The African Child* (1953), perhaps the earliest of this novelistic form, is a classic example of a male *Bildungsroman*.

Kenneth Harrow (1994) perceives this literary type as a springboard for later African novelists and further observes that, 'the European impact on African culture, [is] highlighted in *L'Enfant noir* through Laye's dilemma over choosing to complete his education rather than become a goldsmith like his father' (p. 35). Novels of development share common features. Harrow identifies these as including a clearly defined point of departure, a point of view focalized through a narrator, a defined space incorporating the protagonist's relationship with others (family) and the use of the first person narrative viewpoint (pp. 38–41). These are important analytical points for the *Bildungsroman* tradition.

The significance of the female writer to this tradition is important, especially since male writers rarely explore the implications of gender-imposed limitations on women. Obviously, male writers relate only tangentially to the female predicament in their novels. Indeed, Florence Stratton (1994) notes that 'the female *Bildungsroman* stands in opposition to the entire African male literary tradition – a tradition to which the very notion of female development is alien. For it is a form which, by its very definition, characterizes women as active and dynamic – as developing' (p. 107). Thus the passive, dependent and marginal roles generally given to women in the male *Bildungsroman* and the social myths that perpetuate gender bias and inaccurate pictures of African womanhood have been largely debunked by the female perspective. As a matter of urgency, the female novel of development has given voice to the silent figures of male fiction. More attention is given to the female experience – thoughts, feelings, and actions. Therefore, the popularity of this form among female writers is evidenced by the spate of novels coming out of Africa since the seventies. Among these are Zaynab Alkali's *The Stillborn* (1985), Tsitsi Dangarembga's *Nervous Conditions* (1988), Buchi Emecheta's *Second-Class Citizen* (1975), *The Bride Price* (1976).[5]

As in the male novel of development, the education of the heroine is an important theme for the African female writer. This becomes an arena of conflict and struggle for the heroine seeking educational advancement as a pathway to independence. By virtue of her gender, such aspiration usually creates schisms between the heroine and her family. Undoubtedly, gender becomes the intersecting point between the heroine's educational aspirations and the roles assigned to her by tradition.[6] The embedded conflict is usually the focus of the writer's artistic exploration.

Overall, African novels of development essentially portray patriarchy's mechanisms for creating gender identity. As Buchi Emecheta's *The Bride Price* and Tsitsi Dangarembga's *Nervous Conditions* demonstrate, female socialization is critical in the making of gender-identity. Their visions of childhood capture the dynamics of female socialization into traditional roles.

## Gender identity in the making

Feminists, gender theorists and literary critics have toyed with the definition of woman. They have also argued variously on gender, and its implications for women. Is gender a biological or social construct? What makes woman 'female' and therefore subordinate or second class? Is it biological attributes that determine gender identity or woman's social position in patriarchy? A feminist (western) critic observes that a key concept in feminist theory is 'the distinction between biological sex on the one hand, and socially constructed gender on the other . . . the recognition that, while the sex of the individual depends on anatomy, gender is a culturally constructed artefact' (Palmer, 1989, p. 13). How applicable is this Euro-Western feminist concept to the African woman's cultural situation noting for instance, the problem of essentializing all women into a universally dominated entity?[7] Indeed, a female anthropologist (African) has shown how gender was employed in an African society as an ideological construct to achieve political equity and balance prior to colonialism.[8]

> The fact that biological sex did not always correspond to ideological gender meant that women could play roles usually monopolized by men, or be classified as 'males' in terms of power and authority over others. As such roles were not rigidly masculinized or feminized, no stigma was attached to breaking gender rules. (Amadiume, 1987, p. 185)

What role then does socialization play in gender identity? In *Becoming A Woman: The Socialization of Gender*, Bernice Lott (1991), defines socialization thus:

> the process of learning those behaviors that are appropriate for members of a particular group distinguished from others on the basis of certain ascribed and/or achieved status. The behaviors we learn as appropriate for women in a particular culture and at a particular time constitute the role identified with our sex. Because these behaviors are, in very large part, unrelated to the reliable biological distinctions between the sexes, the word 'gender' is used to identify our learned definitions of women and men (p. 6)

Arguing that the making of gender identity is a life-long process that starts at birth, Lott emphasizes how women are, 'socialized by myths and realities, expectations and responsibilities, sanctions and beliefs, frustrations and satisfactions' (p. xi). Since all women share similar experiences in patriarchy her definition of socialization as a learning process is applicable to women in African societies. This process is manifested in such things as the choice of names for male and female children, the apportionment of domestic duties among male and female children in a household, or the involvement of male children in specific customary rites. Indeed, the importance of naming in gender socialization could be underestimated. For instance, Ali Mazrui (1993), expounding on the gender problem in Africa, categorizes the culture of naming babies as a case of 'benign sexism', which, 'acknowledges gender differences without bestowing sexual advantages or inflicting a gender cost' (p. 89). Remarkably, and contrary to his controversial views on sexism and gender, socialization of the female is observably inculcated through the culture of naming. Thus, 'Nneka' (mother is supreme) that is perceived to 'celebrate womanhood', in reality only idealizes motherhood, underlining it as the pinnacle of female attainment. Examples given by Mazrui from the Igbo society such as 'Nwanyibuife' (woman is something), 'Nwanyibuego' (woman is wealth), do not extol womanhood as he implies. Rather, they objectify women and hint at female commodification while underscoring marriage as the ultimate goal of woman.[9]

The *Bride Price* and *Nervous Conditions* are self-referential portraits in terms of style and setting.[10] As female writers from Africa, the meeting point for Emecheta and Dangarembga lies in their vision of female development in patriarchy. Despite the years separating the two novelists (Emecheta occupies the position of literary foremother to Dangarembga), both share similarities in their cultural experience of patriarchal dominance. For instance, the story of Aku-nna is autobiographical to a certain degree. For both, marriage was a pivotal issue as Ernest Emenyonu (1996) also observes:

> In a personal way, Emecheta draws a parallel between herself and the fictional Aku-nna and contends that she feels convinced that, like Aku-nna, her own marriage broke up because she did not allow her prospective husband to pay her bride price. Aku-nna's bride price was not paid as custom demanded; therefore she had to die (p. 257)

Other parallels between Aku-nna and Emecheta have also been identified by Marie Umeh (1996) such as the privilege of education given to their brothers. Similar to Aku-nna's separation from her father (through death), and psychological distancing from her mother upon her remarriage, Emecheta experienced separation from her biological parents at age nine. Like Aku-nna's mother, Emecheta's mother was inherited by her uncle. At critical moments of despair, both took self-actualizing actions that changed the course of their lives. Aku-nna through her elopement and marriage to a social outcast and Emecheta through appropriating her benefactor's food money to pay for a scholarship application and entrance examination to high school.[11]

Dangarembga's Zimbabwean society is strongly patriarchal, and as Flora Veit-Wild (1987) remarks, women face formidable obstacles especially in matters of education and decision-making.[12] Through the prism of childhood, both authors explore the dilemma faced by many African girls, thereby exposing the vicious cycle of conflict identified by Veit-Wild as 'the expectations of tradition and the extended family on one hand and their own individual feelings on the other' (p. 177). The evidence of this conflict in the two novels affirms my notion of a gendered childhood.

## Education versus gender identity

Education is critical to female independence. Socially, and often symbolically, it transports women beyond the reach of traditional shackles. In the female *Bildungsroman*, women's education challenges patriarchal expectations, sometimes placing the heroine in the role of an iconoclast. As female, Aku-nna's experience of social bias towards her education underlines her disadvantaged status as female. Struggling against traditional impositions, restrictions, and prejudices she 'escapes' the limited world of her childhood, attaining adulthood with greater awareness of herself and society. However, it is an awareness that does not bear positive fruit since she allows herself to be overwhelmed by the psychological hold of tradition.

In *The Bride Price*, the tension between female education and gender socialization is first mentioned by Auntie Matilda in Lagos after Ezekiel's burial. In sympathy for Aku-nna's plight, she remarks; 'The pity of it all, is that they will marry her off very quickly in order to get enough money to pay Nna-nndo's school fees' (*BP*, p. 38); thus making clear that her brother's education is of priority concern. This conflict is further realized within the extended family set-up headed by her uncle, Okonkwo, where her educational advancement causes the male members to be antagonistic towards her. Okonkwo does not value female education; rather he tolerates it because it improves his chances of acquiring a fat bride wealth, a booty that he (and his sons) counts on for social success.

This tension is also present in *Nervous Conditions*. Dangarembga demonstrates through Tambu's story the oppressive facets of patriarchy and the psychological schism it manifests within the female child in particular. As I noted in an earlier paper, this division is metaphorically expressed in the title of the novel, 'nervous conditions' (Uwakweh, 1995, p. 78). Between Tambu and her family, education is a source of conflict. The adult Tambu recalls her childhood experience of gender bias in education. She blames patriarchy, maintaining that in her family the women were an insignificant minority whose needs were often ignored or considered unimportant. Tambu regrets that at thirteen years of age (when her brother Nhamo died), she was still in standard three instead of five solely because her brother was privileged by virtue of his gender. Her educational growth suffers not because she is stupid, but because Nhamo, being male, has the benefits of the scarce financial resources of their parents.

> The needs and sensibilities of the women in my family were not considered a priority, or even legitimate. That was why I was in Standard Three in the year that Nhamo died, instead of in Standard Five, as I should have been by that age. In those days I felt the injustice of my situation every time I thought about it, which I could not help but do often since children are always talking about their age. Thinking about it, feeling the injustice of it, this is how I came to dislike my brother, and not only my brother: my father, my mother – in fact everybody. (*NC*, p. 12)

Tambu's father insists that she learn domestic affairs in line with the socially ascribed role for females, 'Can you cook books and feed them to your husband? Stay at home with your mother. Learn to cook and clean.

Grow vegetables' (*NC*, p. 15). Tambu's first lesson in independence is cultivating a maize field, an action that wins her temporary control over her educational aspirations. She rejects marginality by centralizing her needs. When she 'earns' a donation from an old white lady in Umtali town for her school fees, her father's claim to the money emphasizes female powerlessness to control or shape her destiny. He argues that Tambu is a girl who would one day 'meet a young man and I will have lost everything' (*NC*, p. 30). Tambu's perception of her father's ideas about what is natural and unnatural is clearly defined thus:

> He did not like to see me over absorbed in intellectual pursuits. He became very agitated after he had found me several times reading the sheet of newspaper in which the bread from magrosa had been wrapped as I waited for the sadza to thicken. He thought I was emulating my brother, that the things I read would fill my mind with impractical ideas, making me quite useless for the real tasks of feminine living. (*NC*, pp. 33–34)

Ironically, Nhamo's sudden death offers Tambu the unexpected opportunity to grow intellectually under her uncle Babamukuru's tutelage. She comes to see her sojourn at the mission house as 'the period of my reincarnation', attributing her expanding horizon to the advantage of her cousin Nyasa's library.

## The ultimate goal

Both novels explore female experience at the edge of womanhood. Whereas Tambu is eight years (age of cognition) at the start of her story, Aku-nna is thirteen years and pubescent. In *The Bride Price*, Emecheta projects female socialization into passivity, dependence, and submissiveness. Aku-nna, thirteen years at the beginning of her story, is one of two children. The author shows how this process of socialization begins at birth (as shown in the culture of naming), hinting at the outset that as female, her parents value her primarily for the bride price she will fetch upon her marriage. At birth, 'he (Ezekiel Odia) had named her Aku-nna, meaning literally "father's wealth", knowing that the only consolation he could count on from her would be her bride price' (*BP*, p. 10). Underlying his choice of name for his daughter is socialization into the ethics of ultimate female attainment. Female socialization into marriage is expressed in other respects. Feminine decorum such as in the art of sitting or the expressions of emotion are particularly encouraged in girl children. The incident of her father's funeral ceremony is an example. Aku-nna was encouraged to cry longer than her brother Nna-nndo because 'girls were supposed to exhibit more emotion' (*BP*, p. 30).

Aku-nna bears a double burden by the single act of marriage. Both Ma Blackie's plans of college for her son Nna-nndo, and the burden of raising the entire Odia family from poverty to wealth rest on her shoulders. Intent on finishing school, Aku-nna maintains secrecy about her menstruation – a symbolic act of resistance against forced and early marriage. Thus, she creates for herself a niche, a seemingly secure but fragile world in which only she exercises full control. She alone (and of course Chike) holds the secret of her menstruation, information needed by the outer world dominated by her uncle Okonkwo to seal her marital destiny. By her action, Aku-nna attempts to protect her dreams or aspiration for an education. The narrative voice indicates that, 'it was not that she shrank from becoming an adult, but she was afraid of what her people might force the future to hold for her' (*BP*, p. 104).

Both Emecheta and Dangarembga emphasize the significance of menstruation as a rite of passage to womanhood and, more importantly, underline the restrictive social myths surrounding this biological phenomenon of femaleness. While demonstrating sexual identity, it also determines female eligibility for marriage. Ironically enough, parents look forward to this event in the life of their daughters, while the pubescent child shows concern, anxiety, or even fear about this natural occurrence. As Emecheta demonstrates, part of this fear is tied up with the numerous negative social myths surrounding woman's blood.

In many ways restrictive for the female, the myths surrounding menstruation cut across cultural and historical boundaries. Lott observes that 'next to the incestual taboo, the most potent and lasting of gynarchic taboos is that connected with "woman's blood". Cultural prohibitions include those against cooking food for men, sexual intercourse, religious participation, contact with men preparing for battle or a hunt . . .'.[13]

Though the onset of menstruation signifies both the protagonists' coming of age, Tambu and Aku-nna respond to this natural phenomenon differently. Ironically, and despite the fanfare attending the family's discovery of Aku-nna's state, (she is presented with a live hen by her uncle), the myths and taboos surrounding menstruation (crossing a stream, for example) weight heavily on her mind, robbing her of the joys of womanhood.

While for Aku-nna it foreshadowed early marriage, and an end to her educational aspirations, for Tambu it is the conflict of dealing with a modern feminine hygiene method at the mission house, one that poses a threat to her imbibed notions of female virginity. Confronting a tampon for the first time, Tambu's conflict is apparent:

Did it really look like that inside? I examined a tampon, from the outside only without removing the wrapper because I did not want to waste one, and considered aloud the consequences of pushing the offensively shaped object into my vagina, but Nyasa laughed at me and teased me. She said I was better off losing my virginity to a tampon, which wouldn't gloat over its achievement, than to a man, who would add mine to his hoard of hymens. (*NC*, p. 96)

Marriage does not pose any immediate threat for Tambu; but it lurks behind the insinuations and expectations of her father and generous uncle as the ultimate female goal. Indeed, Tambu questions the restrictive hold of marriage on her life as a female:

> Marriage. I had nothing against it in principle. In an abstract way I thought it was a very good idea. But it was irritating the way it always cropped up in one form or another, stretching its tentacles back to bind me before I had even begun to think about it seriously, threatening to disrupt my life before I could even call it my own. (*NC*, p. 180)

## Sexual codes

An aspect of gender socialization is embedded in the sexual codes of the authors' settings thereby underscoring patriarchy's manipulation of female sexuality. The desirability of male sexuality transcends the cultural moral code of chastity. Sexual expressivity is undesirable in the female but condoned in the male. Only the female bears the burden of the 'moral albatross', by way of enforced virginity.[14] Umeh aptly observes that, 'chastity and sexual demure is the measure of a good woman's moral character' (p. 194). This code operates in *The Bride Price* in the custom of presenting a blood-stained cloth to a bride's parents as indicative of chastity. This custom enforces the sexual code among Ibuza females. Ma Blackie's diatribe on Aku-nna illustrates two contradictory sexual ethics in a single setting:

> You mean you have nice breasts and don't want men to touch? Girls like you tend to end up having babies in their father's houses, because they cannot endure open play, so they go to secret places and have themselves disvirgined. Is that the type of person you are turning out to be? I will kill you if you bring shame and dishonour on us. How can he hurt you with all these others watching? (*BP*, p. 121)

Furthermore, among the Ibuza, Emecheta shows how male privileges are endorsed by tradition. Forced marriage is sanctioned by the custom of abduction, or cutting a lock of hair from the victim. Enforced virginity and its verification at marriage appears to have been socially instituted for male ego gratification. (Interestingly, Aku-nna plays on this traditional male ego booster to win her escape from an unpleasant union with Okoboshi). Okoboshi's parents are aware of his indulgences but never curb him. Chike's sexual escapades are numerous. In fact, there are suggestions that his first interest in Aku-nna may have been purely sexual rather than genuine. Okonkwo's teenage sons seek out their sweethearts openly. Okoboshi makes sexual overtures to Aku-nna in her mother's presence and her protest against his liberties is roundly condemned by her mother, Ma Blackie. The authorial voice adds that, 'in Ibuza every young man was entitled to his fun', but the blame usually went to the girls, thus chastity is esteemed as the apex of feminine decorum. 'A girl who had had adventures before marriage was never respected in her new home; everyone in the village would know about her past, especially if she was unfortunate enough to be married to an egocentric man' (*BP*, p. 84).

In *Nervous Conditions*, two distinct forms of socialization are also evident between Tambu and her brother, Nhamo. This is also true of Nyasa and Chido. Tambu finds Nhamo's display of male superiority very obnoxious. For example, Nhamo has distinct views about male privileges and female inferiority and does not fail to demonstrate his authority over his sisters. It is also interesting how his parents and society at large reinforce gender identity. Tambu recounts that when Nhamo comes home from the mission school, fowls are killed for him even though the family rarely indulges itself in such a luxury. Again, her uncle Babamukuru's expectations of his daughter, Nyasa, differ from that of the son, Chido. In spite of his educational attainment, his notions of traditional femininity complement those of the larger society. This creates friction between father and rebellious daughter that explodes to a physical conflict, thus allowing Tambu more insight into the female problem. She observes:

> and thinking how dreadfully familiar that scene had been, with Babamukuru condemning Nyasa to whoredom, making her a victim of her femaleness, just as I had felt victimised at home in the days when Nhamo went to school and I grew my maize. The victimization, I saw, was universal. It didn't depend on poverty, on lack of education or on tradition. It didn't depend on any of the things I had thought it depended on. Men took it everywhere with them. Even heroes like Babamukuru did it. And that was the problem. You had to admit that Nyasa had no tact. You had to admit she was altogether too volatile and strong-willed. You couldn't ignore the fact that she had no respect for Babamukuru when she ought to have had lots of it. But what I didn't like was the way all the conflicts came back to this question of femaleness. Femaleness as opposed and inferior to maleness. (*NC*, pp. 115–116)

## Conclusion

The significance of gender-socialization in the African female *Bildungsroman* delineates the essence of patriarchal societies, as well as its influence on the female child's formative years. Gender-based socialization as portrayed in the novels creates a plethora of feelings in the female child ranging from ambivalence to equivocation or rebellion against social tenets. Each of our protagonists (Aku-nna and Tambu) in her own peculiar ways tries to carve a haven in which to escape the realities of her femaleness. Tambu initiates and cultivates a maize field to earn her tuition. She says to her father, 'If you will give me some seed, I will clear my own field and grow my own maize. Not much. Just enough for the fees' (*NC*, p. 17). For Tambu, Maiguru's educational achievement, lifestyle, and freedom from the drudgery of domesticity inspired her to escape from the threat of her own mother's condition and poverty. Nyasa seeks refuge in anorexia, exploring her temporary control over herself.

On Aku-nna's part, she maintains secrecy about her menstruation to delay marriage and fulfil her educational aspirations. Though this hope was cut short by her abduction and forced marriage, she extricates herself from a traditionally sanctioned marriage, preferring to be a social outcast by her union with Chike Ofulue. Though the manner of the protagonists' escapes differ, the comparable nature of the experiences of female children is nonetheless rooted in patriarchy, and its concomitant gender bias. Both characters suffer bouts of guilt for stepping outside the bounds of traditional role ascription. Tambu for example is tormented by 'dreams' of deserting her female role as her educational career progresses. For Aku-nna, this guilt is marked by her internalization of Ibuza tradition and its psychological hold over those who step outside its bounds. One could, in fact, compare Aku-nna's equivocation to Tambu's fierce presence of mind, and her extreme sensitivity toward her social limitations as female. No wonder she survives to 'voice' her story; while Aku-nna dies, thereby maintaining the social myths that limit female growth and challenge.

The female *Bildungsroman* provides an important insight into the dynamics of gender construction in patriarchy. Emecheta's and Dangarembga's visions of gendered childhood share similarities that indeed emphasize the necessity of cross-cultural perspectives on the making of gender identity. This is important for determining both the sources and areas of conflict in gender-based socialization for the female in various cultures. As feminist cross-cultural proponents note, it would enhance the comparison and evaluation of social policy, the illumination of shared phenomenon among women, and the generation of feminist theory applicable to women worldwide.[15]

---

## NOTES

1. Ifi Amadiume, *Male Daughters, Female Husbands: Gender and Sex in an African Society*, (New Jersey: Zed Books, 1987). Amadiume argues that 'Western culture and Christian religion brought by colonialism carried rigid gender ideologies which aided and supported the exclusion of women from power hierarchy, whether in government or the church in the modern society.' p. 185.

2. Brenda Berrian, *Bibliography of African Women Writers and Journalists (Ancient Egypt–1984)*, (Washington, D.C.: Three Continents, 1985). Entries include 'a total of 386 authors of folklore and creative literary works and 74 journalists . . . from North, East, West, Central and Southern Africa.' p. x.

3. Ali Mazrui, 'The Black Woman and the Problem of Gender: An African Perspective,' *Research in African Literatures* 24.1 (1993): 103.

4. Florence Stratton, *Contemporary African Literature and the Politics of Gender*, (New York: Routledge, 1994). Stratton points out that gender as a social and analytic category has been ignored in African literature. p. 1.

5. The story of *The Bride Price* was first written by Emecheta when she joined her husband in London at age 17. The manuscript was subsequently burnt by the husband. Critics have noted parallels between this novel and her autobiographical *Second-Class Citizen*. On these bases, *The Bride Price* shares in the literary tradition of the *Bildungsroman*.

6. Other intersecting points apart from gender are patriarchy, race, class, colonialism, imperialism. These offer varying perspectives to women's struggles worldwide. See, for example, Cheryl Johnson-Odim, 'Common Themes, Different Contexts: Third World Women and Feminism, '*Third World Women and The Politics of Feminism*, eds Chandra Mohanty, Ann Russo, and Lourdes Torres. (Bloomington: Indiana UP, 1991): 314.

7. In 'Cartographies of Struggle: Third World Women and the Politics of Feminism,' Chandra Mohanty warns against essentialist notions of Third World feminist struggles, while positing the idea of an 'imagined community' of women united along political rather than biological or cultural lines. p. 4.

8. Amadiume's study, spanning three historical periods, is specific to the Nnobi (Igbo) community, and analyses women's status in this socio-cultural system. p. 185.

9. In this article, 'The Black Woman and the Problem of Gender: An African Perspective', *Research in African Literatures* 24.1 (1993): 87, Mazrui categorises sexism into three: benevolent, benign, and malignant. In his classification, the culture of naming babies falls under benign or harmless sexism. In response, Molara Ogundipe-Leslie faults Mazrui's reductive theoretical perspective on gender in 'Beyond Hearsay and Academic Journalism: The Black Woman and Ali Mazrui' *Research in African Literatures* 24.1 (1993): 105–112.

10. Although *The Bride Price* does not use the first person narrative viewpoint as *Nervous Conditions* does, the 'illusion of mimesis' is created in the discourse pattern through focalization shifts from Aku-nna's perspective to that of the major narrator who functions as 'Ibuza ethnographer and anti-traditionalist ideologue'. See Genevieve Slomski, 'Dialogue in the Discourse: A Study of Revolt in Selected Fiction by African Women.' diss. Indiana U., 1989: 63.

11. Marie Umeh, '(En) Gendering African Womanhood: Locating Sexual Politics in Igbo Society and Across Boundaries', *Emerging Perspectives on Buchi Emecheta*, 1996, p. xxv.

12. In 'Creating a New Society: Women's Writing in Zimbabwe' *The Journal of Commonwealth Literature*, 22.1 (1987): 172–3, Flora Veit-Wild identifies the following as obstacles women face in patriarchy: lack of education, male prejudice and arrogance, sexism in publishing.

13. Bernice Lott citing Elizabeth Davis (1972) in *Becoming A Woman: the Socialization of Gender*, (Springfield, Illinois: C. C. Thomas, 1991) p. 105.

14. Marie Umeh acknowledges Tuzyline Allan as the source for the term in this article, 'Procreation Not Recreation: decoding Mama in Buchi Emecheta's *The Joys of Motherhood*,' *Emerging Perspectives*, 1996, p. 191.

15. Shulamit Reinharz, *Feminist Methods in Social Research*, (New York: Oxford University, 1992), p. 113

# WORKS CITED

Alkali, Zaynab. *The Stillborn.* London: Longman Drumbeat, 1984.

Amadiume, Ifi. *Male Daughters, Female Husbands: Gender and Sex in an African Society.* New Jersey: Zed Books, 1987.

Brown, Lloyd. *Woman Writers in Black Africa.* Westport, CT: Greenwood Press, 1981.

Dangarembga, Tsitsi. *Nervous Conditions.* Seattle, Washington: The Seal Press, 1988.

Emecheta, Buchi. *The Bride Price.* Glasgow: Fontana, 1978.

—— *Second-Class Citizen.* New York: George Braziller, 1975.

Emenyonu, Ernest. 'Technique and Language in Buchi Emecheta's *The Bride Price, The Slave Girl,* and *The Joys of Motherhood.'* *Emerging Perspectives on Buchi Emecheta.* Ed. Marie Umeh. Trenton, New Jersey: Africa World Press, 1996. 251–65.

Harrow, Kenneth. *Thresholds of Change in African Literature: The Emergence of a Tradition.* Portsmouth, NH: Heinemann, 1994.

Johnson-Odim, Cheryl. 'Common Themes, Different Contexts: Third World Women and Feminism'. *Third World Women and the Politics of Feminism.* Eds Chandra Mohanty, Ann Russo, and Lourdes Torres. Bloomington: Indiana University Press, 1991. 314–47.

Laye, Camara. *The African Child (L'Enfant Noir,* 1953). London: Fontana, 1959.

Lott, Bernice. *Becoming a Woman: The Socialization of Gender.* Springfield, Illinois: C. C. Thomas, 1991.

Mazrui, Ali. 'The Black Woman and The Problem of Gender: An African Perspective'. *Research in African Literatures* 24.1 (1993): 87–104.

Mohanty, Chandra. 'Cartographies of Struggle: Third World Women and The Politics of Feminism'. *Third World Women and the Politics of Feminism,* 1–47.

Ogundipe-Leslie, Molara. 'Beyond Hearsay and Academic Journalism: The Black Woman and Ali Mazrui'. *Research in African Literatures* 24.1 (1993): 105–12.

Palmer, Paulina. *Contemporary Women's Fiction: Narrative Practice and Feminist Theory.* London: University Press of Mississippi, 1989.

Reinharz, Shulamit. *Feminist Methods in Social Research.* New York: Oxford University Press, 1992.

Slomski, Genevieve. 'Dialogue in the Discourse: A Study of Revolt in Selected Fiction by African Women'. diss. Indiana. 1989.

Stratton, Florence. *Contemporary African Literature and the Politics of Gender.* New York: Routledge, 1994.

Umeh, Marie. '(En) Gendering African Womanhood: Locating Sexual Politics in Igbo Society and Across Boundaries'. *Emerging Perspectives,* 1996: xxiii–xlii.

—— 'Procreation Not Recreation: Decoding Mama in Buchi Emecheta's *The Joys of Motherhood'. Emerging Perspectives,* 1996: 189–206.

Uwakweh, Pauline. 'Debunking Patriarchy: The Liberational Quality of Voicing in Tsitsi Dangarembga's *Nervous Conditions'. Research in African Literatures* 26.1 (1995): 75–84.

Veit-Wild, Flora. 'Creating a New Society: Women's Writing in Zimbabwe.' *The Journal of Commonwealth Literatures.* 22.1 (1987): 171–8.

Gender Issues
in Zaynab Alkali's Novels

Adetayo Alabi

Zaynab Alkali, the acclaimed writer and winner of the 1985 Association of Nigerian Authors' award for prose fiction with her first novel, *The Stillborn*, is one of the first female novelists from northern Nigeria. Her arrival on the male-dominated Nigerian literary scene was welcomed enthusiastically. Her widely-read novels focus on the position of the African woman in patriarchal Africa. She creates various characters who represent different strands of the ongoing debate about the relationship between the African woman and her male counterparts. While some of her characters are able to launch an assault on the object position allotted to the African woman in colonial texts like Joseph Conrad's *Heart of Darkness* and some early African novels and chart a new subject position of their own, others reproduce the subservient stereotype of the African woman.

In broad terms, the dialogue in Alkali's *The Stillborn* and *The Virtuous Woman* can be situated within the overall discourse of African literature. Since this discourse is fundamentally sociological, the conflicts in Alkali's novels are communal. This is in line with Achebe's argument that the 'writer and his society live in the same place' ('The Novelist as Teacher', p. 42); hence 'art is, and was always in the service of man' ('Africa and Her Writers', p. 19). More specifically, the discourse is an interrogation of the role of society in the formation of opinion on gender issues. It discusses how society dictates the behavioural pattern of characters towards gender matters, why some characters accept society's conservative posture on gender unquestionably, and why others reject them in various ways.

Like Ngugi's *Devil on the Cross*, Saadawi's *Woman at Point Zero*, and Aidoo's *Anowa*, the protagonists of Alkali's *The Stillborn* and *The Virtuous Woman* are female. The difference between them, however, lies in the manipulation of their energy to resist or accept gender inequality. While Wariinga and Firdaus are able to question patriarchy comprehensively in *Devil on the Cross* and *Woman at Point Zero* respectively, the resistance to patriarchy, though successfully launched, cannot be

22

sustained in *The Stillborn* and *Anowa*. On the other hand, the structure of the dialogue in *The Virtuous Woman* does not allow a forceful feminine voice.

*The Stillborn* and *The Virtuous Woman* are set in a rigidly hierarchical patriarchal society in which the interests of men come before those of women and children and in which childless women are at the bottom of the list. This feature of the society runs through both of Alkali's novels and tremendously affects the positions of the various characters on gender issues. There is largely a division between the private and the public realms in the society (a division that some scholars have established as a reinforcement of gender exploitation) so that while men operate in the outside economy, women are restricted largely to the home. This is the case when Li in (*The Stillborn*) visits Habu Adams in the city. After the men go out to work, the women take their time in getting ready for the day (p. 70).

The novels are set in a community where women's feelings towards men are supposed to be bottled up as Awa demonstrates in the meeting with Habu Adams at the dancing arena. She plays to the dictates of the society regarding traditional courtship. She is not supposed to show any interest in a man when they have just met. She is supposed to measure the man's seriousness by his persistence despite her uncooperative attitude towards him. Also, a woman is not expected to tell a man boldly about her feelings for him or be part of the decision-making process in a relationship. This is why Li does not go to see Habu Adams after their baby is born. She keeps on waiting for him to come for her. In addition, because the society regards a man as 'superior' to a woman, Baba can beat Awa with little uneasiness, regardless of her age, but not Sule, his first son (*The Stillborn*, p. 23).

The setting of these novels is a society where marriage and children are of supreme importance. This is why, despite Li's assertiveness, she is still contained in the marital institution as she decides to go back to her husband eventually despite the crisis their earlier encounter engendered. Because of the preference for male children Dogo abandons his wife because she has only one son and many daughters (*The Virtuous Woman*, p. 47). Daughters also passively acquiesce in this discrimination and accept the position of second fiddle. Ironically however, this patriarchal society respects education, especially for women. Nana in *The Virtuous Woman* is envied by everybody, and Hajjo and Laila, like their father and their village chief, are very proud of their admission to Her Majesty's School.

It is against this patriarchal background that Li's assertiveness (*The Stillborn*) can be situated and analysed. Her uniqueness comes out clearly very early. At birth, she does not cry like a 'normal' child, and she 'came with the bag of waters intact' (p. 6). Her appearance is also unusual. Her hair is 'kinky' like an adult's and her eyes are 'like Old

Yakumba's' while her ears look like they have no holes in them. Her name at birth was Mwapu but people call her Li – shortened form for Libra – because of her counter-hegemonic tendencies. The strangeness foregrounded at birth is developed as she grows. On completing primary school, she misses the freedom of her boarding school, and questions their rather oppressive and stifling family environment. Her younger siblings are too young to join her in protesting their confinement. Her only ally is Sule, her older brother. Her questioning tendency goes a step further when she breaks her father's fence to attend Pa Dawi's funeral contrary to custom. This trend of resistance is, however, rebuked by the conservative society as the discussion between Mariama and Audu shows. They do not see any reason why Li should resist any restrictions imposed on her by her family, and this gradually affects her and leads ultimately to a reduction in her revolutionary vigour.

Catherine Acholonu argues that *The Stillborn* 'is essentially a vehement registration of a feminist discontent which is at once dynamic, fiercely radical, positively revolutionary and therefore progressive'. Acholonu's position can be sustained up to the time Habu Adams marries Li. The story is, however, different from this point because Li abandons her radical approach to inequality and changes from a positively aggressive woman to a quiet day dreamer who waits for a husband for four years. It is noteworthy that just as this marriage marks the stillbirth of Li's vision, it is also connected with the turning point in Habu's ambition of being a doctor to a salesman. It is at this point that Li concedes superiority to the man. As the narrator puts it, '[f] or four years she had yearned to be in her husband's house. She had dreamt of the moments when *she would cook his meals wash his clothes and cuddle him to her breasts*' (p. 69, emphasis mine). One of the effects of Li's uncritical longing for Habu Adams and her acceptance of an inferior position relative to him is that her potential for asserting and developing a counter vision for the society, a vision of gender equality, is aborted. This is further reinforced by her unconvincing decision to join her husband who had earlier treated her as an appendage, Habu's incapacitation notwithstanding. Even Awa, her less critical sister, is surprised at Li's decision: 'This wasn't the sister she was used to, impetuous and critical of people. This was a different Li, tolerant and understanding' (p. 94). The new Li is substantially different from the Li that told Habu off earlier after having been abandoned by him. Omolara Ladele's opinion that there is 'a serious contradiction, indeed self-negation in Li' is therefore very apt.

Li's education after her initial separation from Habu Adams, though remarkable in a situation where woman's education is the exception rather than the rule, does not really help matters. She decides to go to school as Amina Mama suggests because of 'the hatred and jealousy of other women rather than any resourcefulness'. In addition, her education does not provide her with the tools to further develop her understanding of gender inequality. Furthermore, her efforts in her parents' house after Baba's death are still within this scheme. She rises to the challenges of the time simply because there is no 'man' in the house since Sule has been disowned.

Just as Seiyifa Koroye argues, Awa and Faku 'stand as foils in their different ways' to Li (p. 50). Though Awa is older than Li, she is more compromised and contented. In line with patriarchal demands, she gets married to Dan Fiama, the village headmaster, but their dream of upgrading the school with Fiama as principal and Awa as the head of the adult education unit is unfulfilled. Fiama becomes disorientated and he who 'used to be the best there was in the village' (p. 87) becomes the 'chief alcoholic' (p. 86) and 'lost his head in the bottles' (p. 82). Awa, therefore, leaves for home to fulfil the conventional dream of procreation.

Just as Li is initially displaced in Habu's house, Faku is also dehumanized in Garba's where she is only a second wife. Garba, like his friend 'who keeps four women in four different areas of the city' (p. 45), belongs to the school that sees women as properties to be acquired. Faku, however, leaves Garba's house 'for some other town and is deep in prostitution' (p. 93). According to Li, 'if any of us didn't mean to drift, it was Faku' (p. 100). Later in life, however, she becomes a social worker (p. 102).

Unlike *The Stillborn, The Virtuous Woman* does not have a strong female character. Nana Ai, Laila, and Hajjo who are students going to Her Majesty School in Kudu do not possess the energy to scrutinize the position of the woman in their society. *The Virtuous Woman*, therefore, operates almost exclusively within the realm of the phallocratic depiction of the female characters. For example, Nana, who is 'quiet and good natured' regrets being a female from to time: '[p]erhaps she said to herself, if I were a male, I would be a doctor' (p. 10). She sees a man as a superior; hence, as far as she is concerned, a man should help out when there are problems as in the car mishap. She is not aggressive but coy, not boisterous but quiet, not assertive but compromising; hence she is 'the virtuous woman whose price is far above rubies'. Unlike Li in *The Stillborn* who tries to question gender exploitation, Nana does not. She accepts the gender roles assigned to her by the society without reservation. This is why she is 'the virtuous woman' from the perspective of her patriarchal society. Ladele raises a very important question in relation to Nana's virtuous woman medal which is 'whether traditionalism and conservativism as encapsulated in Nana are really virtuous especially at a time when contemporary women are striving to free themselves of the oppressive traditional (male oriented) perception of women'. The few gains for gender equality championed by people like Li are sacrificed and not developed further by characters like Nana.

Laila, though relatively assertive, like Nana, does not transcend the stereotypical image of the African woman in *The Virtuous Woman*. In fact, she reinforces it. While Hajjo, her cousin, 'had passed the Common Entrance Examination in class six, Laila had barely made it after repeating three times in different classes. She might be clever in some other things but not in the classroom' (p. 6). Perhaps she is 'clever' in her acceptance of a submissive role to the man. She 'falls in love' easily with the likes of Abubakar who 'flaunted his riches' (p. 56) and for economic reasons with 'the man in Army uniform' almost as soon as Abubakar dies. She is disappointed that the man does not want her. This prostitute-like image is also evident in her scheme to paint her body in order to attract a lift for herself and her colleagues from male drivers. Hajjo, Laila's cousin, does not come out of the text as a forceful character of any sort, being only discussed as an addition to Nana and Laila. She admires Nana and enjoys her company, unlike Laila who feels threatened by her. She is hardworking but lacking self-will, dances to whatever tune Laila plays.

As noted earlier, Li's is the most developed character in *The Stillborn* and *The Virtuous Woman*. She sets out to launch an attack on gender inequality. Her assertiveness gives way, however, because of the pressures around her and because of the staunch patriarchal society she lives in. She is, therefore, contained in the marital institution that she works really hard to make responsive to her position as a woman. She remains remarkably interesting especially when viewed in relation to the change in her initial trend of resistance to gender inequalities. The change from the uncompromising to the lethargic Li, therefore, shows that fundamentally, not a lot has changed in the literary depiction of the African woman here. She is still an appendage to the man and still determined by him. It is, however, important to note that the creation of characters like Li, despite all possible reservations about her development, is still largely revolutionary in her society. This is perhaps why Acholonu's essay cited earlier is titled 'The Woman Comes of Age in the Nigerian Novel: A study of Zaynab Alkali's *The Stillborn*'. Unlike *The Stillborn* which attempts to interrogate the position of the African woman in a patriarchal society, *The Virtuous Woman* takes this position for granted and no serious questioning of the gender issue takes place in the novel.

As I have attempted to show in this paper, Alkali's focus is on her female characters. They are more positively discussed relative to their peripherally positioned male counterparts. Furthermore, just as the girls in *The Virtuous Woman* do not grow into maturity, unlike those in *The Stillborn*, more is said about the men in *The Stillborn* than those in *The Virtuous Woman*. For example, those men discussed in *The Stillborn* live strictly within and promote gender exploitation: Fiama is a drunk, Garba is a chain-smoker, Adams is a wretched villain, and Alhaji Bature is 'a cunny dirty man'. Only Sule and the husband of Adams' landlady are given some positive traits, though these become unimportant when put beside other aspects of their characters. The trend started in *The Stillborn* is only a beginning, a prelude to a more substantial examination of the position of the African woman. It goes to show that this phase is only introductory in terms of subverting patriarchy. For this trend to be more encompassing, it has to avoid any form of reverse discrimination in which male bashing replaces female exploitation and ensure that neither the male nor the female is a victim. Similarly, for this trend to be exhaustive, it has to address other levels of exploitation like racial and class inequality so that one does not perpetuate the other. This is particularly important, as Cora Kaplan puts it because 'a feminist literary criticism which privileges gender in isolation from other forms of social determination offers us a similar partial reading of the role played by sexual difference in literary discourse, a reading bled dry of its most troubling and contradictory meanings' (p. 858).

---

# WORKS CITED

Achebe, Chinua. 'Africa and Her Writers'. *Morning Yet on Creation Day*. London: Heineman Educational Books Limited, 1974, 19–29.

—— 'The Novelist as Teacher'. *Morning Yet on Creation Day*, 42–5.

Acholonu, Rose. 'The Woman Comes of Age in the Nigerian Novel: A Study of Zaynab Alkali's *The Stillborn*'. Paper presented at the 1986 African Literature Association Conference, Michigan State University, East Lansing, USA, 1986.

Aidoo, Ama Ata. *Anowa*. London: Longman Drumbeat, 1970.

Alabi, Adetayo. 'Zaynab Alkali'. *The Routledge Encyclopaedia of Post-Colonial Literatures*. Eds Benson, Eugene and L. W. Conolly, London and New York: Routledge, 1994, 32.

—— 'Zaynab Alkali'. (forthcoming) *The Companion to African Literatures in English*. Eds G. D. Killam & Ruth Rowe.

Alkali, Zaynab. *The Stillborn*. London: Longman, 1984.

—— *The Virtuous Woman*. Nigeria: Longman, 1987.

Bakhtin, M. M. 'Discourse in the Novel'. *The Dialogic Imagination* Trans. Emerson, C. and Holquist M.; Ed. Holquist, M., Austin: University of Texas Press, 1987, 259–422.

Bauer, Dale. 'Gender in Bakhtin's Carnival'. *Feminisms: An Anthology of Literary Theory and Criticism*. Eds Warhol, R. R. and D. P. Herndl, New Brunswick, N.J.: Rutgers UP, 1992, 671–84.

Frank, Katherine. 'Women without Men: The Feminist Novel in Africa'. *Women in African Literature*. 15 (1987): 14–34.

Kaplan, Cora. 'Pandora's Box: Subjectivity, Class and Sexuality in Socialist Feminist Criticism'. *Feminisms: An Anthology of Literary Theory and Criticism*. Eds Warhol, R. R. and D. P. Herndl, New Brunswick, N.J.: Rutgers UP, 1992, 857–77.

Koroye, Seiyifa. 'The Ascetic Feminist Vision of Zaynab Alkali.' *Nigerian Female Writers: A Critical Perspective*. Eds Otokunefor, H. and O. Nwodo, Lagos: Malthouse Publishing Limited, 1989, 47–51.

Ladele, Omolara. 'The Novels of Zaynab Alkali: Another View'. In *The Guardian Literary Series* (GLS) 103. *The Guardian*, 29 August 1987.

Little, Kenneth. *The Sociology of Urban Women's Image in African Literature.* London: Macmillan, 1980.

Mama, Amina. 'The Stillborn, Tale of a Marriage'. (Book Review). *West Africa*, 29 July 1985.

Ngugi wa Thiong'o. *Devil on the Cross.* London: Heinemann Educational Books Limited, 1982.

Ogundipe-Leslie, Molara. 'The Female Writer and Her Commitment'. *Women in African Literature Today*, 15 (1987): 5–13.

Oje-Ade, Femi. 'Female Writers, Male Critics.' *African Literature Today*, 13 158–179 London: James Currey and Trenton: Africa World Press 1983.

Saadawi, Nawal El. *Woman at Point Zero.* London: Zed Books, 1983.

## Maxwell Okolie

Ah yes, all that is so long ago!
how you would like to be young again,
to run down a path once more,
to leap over the Savannah, bursting
with laughter, tumbling against the
others, to play even more energetically
than you did before.
In that way perhaps you could teach
children to realize what play is,
to enjoy more keenly, to appreciate
the good fortune of being a child,
the good fortune they bathe in, but choose
to ignore in their hurry to grow up.[1]
                                    Bernard Dadié

Very few people recall their childhood without a flutter of emotion. This
magic world of innocence and carefreeness echoes profoundly in
African literature. This privileged phase of growing up is often used as
intimate, passion-packed subject matter in fiction. To render poetically
its complex visions was once the yearning of some African novelists
who consider it essential not only to the understanding of African
personality and the 'Negro-world' but also to the remaking of Africa. In
fact the African child did not become a subject of literature until the
early fifties in the wake of negritude controversies. The publication of
Camara Laye's *The African Child* (1954) restates the problem of the
myth of African childhood, and also puts to rest some of the pre-
conceived notions on the matter. To many negritude militants bent, at
the time, on pleading Africa's cause with relentless aggression, Laye's
novel appeared like a total diversion, little short of a 'betrayal' to the
common focus of the moment. This emotional reaction seemed clearly
to have lost sight of the important vista of negritude which Laye had
just opened: namely, childhood as a vital clue to the understanding of
the 'Homo Africanus' and the 'Black Soul'. For Aimé Césaire, 'negritude
is the simple recognition of the fact of being black, of accepting this fact,
of our destiny as black, of our history and our culture'.[2] Basic to this

culture, history and destiny is the childhood that the African passed through. Whatever civilization is to be edified or history to be perpetuated is deeply rooted in it. There, in the values that constitute it, in the crises that traverse or characterize it lies the essence of negritude. In the beginning there was childhood, and childhood makes the man or woman. This is perhaps the vital message that Laye tried to convey. It is only by discovering it, that one could assume it, possibly enrich it, with foreign contacts, if necessary, while actualizing its merits in our ways of life.

Childhood is therefore the foundation stone on which our life is constructed. Although this article does not intend to tackle Laye's *The African Child*, it is however pertinent to point out that Laye set a precedent in discussing the theme in the first place, thus making it possible for subsequent novelists directly or indirectly to integrate it in their works, and so bring into focus in various ways, a more profound and complete psychology of African childhood.

Shrouded in myth, rash generalizations, patent untruths and ethnological insinuations the personality and inner realities of the African child badly needed clarification and highlighting. Often perceived by foreign observers, misinformed tourists and anthropologists as a subject of pity, a victim of environment and therefore a miserable being in a 'hostile' world, African children had to be presented in their true light through the novels, in order to clear such doubts as to whether they have any childhood to remember or savour; whether this childhood is not a 'hell' of penury from which they are trying to escape. It is not for nothing that such authors as Bernard Dadié,[3] and Seydou Badian[4] go to great lengths in their novels to demonstrate how fundamentally African childhood differs in content and physical nature from its Western type and by analysing it with such intimate subtlety and insight they prove that it is unwise to apply the same yardstick of cultural and social determinism to both African and European patterns of life. Today, African children and childhood have become a familiar theme in literature and rightly so, for history, this man-made instrument of domination and oppression, made a common cause with colonization to subject Africans to a mode of evolution not experienced by any other race. The evocation of childhood, whether real or symbolic, for Africans is therefore a psychogenic impulse of self-assertion and self-search.

Condemned by colonization as a people without history, without civilization, without a culture; a people who wrote nothing, invented nothing and contributed nothing to world culture, Africans were fashioned into a sorry image of a 'passenger' without luggage, mere parasite onlookers as the rest of the world passed them by. The greatest agony was that of being reduced to nothing and made to feel so. It was this calculated effort to grossly misrepresent them, their world and values that prompted some African writers to beat a retreat to their 'roots', in order to take a deep and closer look at how their life began, and what quality it held for them. Faced with the demeaning realities of colonial times and the overzealous, newfangled implementations brought about by agents of 'mission civilitrice' to Africa, some of these African novelists, trapped between a disappearing familiar world, and an invidiously pervading Westernism, sought refuge and psychological compensation in the evocation of their childhood. There, in the elysium of their ancestors, in the intimate details of their environment, activities and close relations, they rediscovered the security and confidence that were gradually being eroded by the facts of colonization. There, in their childhood memories are stored the great emotional moments that enriched their lives; reminiscences of joys or disappointments, hidden 'treasures' that gave them a sense of completeness and perfection which colonization was actively busy divesting them of.

It is not surprising that most evocations of childhood assume the tone of a romantic regret of a 'paradise lost'. It is in those terms that Léopold Sédar Senghor talks of the paradise of his African childhood[5] and in spite of many years of sojourn in Europe, in spite of near-perfect assimilation into French culture he still kept intact his 'African soul' nourished by the beauty of African rights and the souvenirs of his childhood Eden where birds swarmed ceaselessly. 'Perfection' says Mircea Eliade, 'lies in the origins'[6], symbol of innocence and state of edenic harmony between man and the cosmos. This perfection belonged to all Africans before the 'fall' brought about by the devouring, conquering hands of colonization. Evocation of childhood is tantamount to a return to this first state of primeval beatitude and splendour characterized by spontaneity and natural simplicity.

To some novelists like Bernard Dadié, Cheikh Hamidou Kane and Ngugi, for example, this return to a childhood universe turned out to be an itinerary of self-search, a balance-sheet of all that made up the alchemy of growing up.

To others, childhood in its dim distant attraction is an alluring treasure house containing the best 'particles' of their lives, dreams, loves, passions; things that time has inexorably carried out of their reach. Consequently recalling childhood experiences amounts to revisiting and reconstructing the self, a remaking of a world with its sensations and events. Man has a way of leaving part of himself behind in the events and experiences that initiate him into existence. By talking or writing about them he gathers himself once more into one undivided entity across time and space. In this way he is able, by this kind of archeological excavation of the past, to see what he used to be that he is no more, or seek deliverance from the snares of a hostile present. The evocation of childhood therefore helps to remould our existence.

Dadié's autobiographical novel, *Climbié* is not just a narration of the facts of life, but an elaborate *processus* of individuation that finally turned him into a protagonist of negritude. In the same way Senghor's defence and illustration of African heritage and culture would have lacked merit if he had not had the benefit of his particular childhood experience to back it up. For him it is an act of reliving his severe childhood in the Sine Kingdom; he recalls not just *'joal'* and its festivities, but also the visits of King Koumbe Ndotene Diouf' to his father with all the pomp that such occasions demanded. Such acts of reminiscence brought back to the distressed African, in a world that was becoming strange with intrusions, a sense of belonging, a familiar ground on which to reassemble all the constitutive elements of himself, being displaced and dispersed by the executors of the civilizing mission in Africa.

One of the greatest implications of childhood in African literature is not its role as a means of recalling the grandeur and valour that characterized the African peoples' past, but as a period of initiation of the child into the mysteries of nature and existence.

Most children grow first of all in the rural world where the white man is rare and where African civilization and tradition still retain their strong natural flavour, moral foundations and human significance. Nature all round the child becomes not just a 'friend and companion', but an open book, a mentor, an encyclopedia of knowledge at the child's disposal. The sky and its clouds, the stars at night, away from the glitter and artificial lights of the cities; the wind, the fauna and flora, the birds, everything has its message, its lessons from which the child benefits through an uncanny art of interpretation acquired living close to nature.

It is this poetic intimacy, an enthralling air of calmness and well-being pervading his childhood surroundings in the farms and in the village, that make Dadié's *Climbié* a moving story of one who understands not just the desires and aspirations of his fellow men but also the language of mute or aphonic things. This education is further enriched with folktales, legends, proverbs with moral overtones illustrating prudence, honesty, generosity, patience, community service, wisdom, fraternal ties: qualities that are considered indispensable to the guidance of mankind and the stability of the society. The child is the parent of tomorrow, and as such is specially prepared for the task ahead, namely perpetuating not just the clan, the traditions, but also the values that give meaning to existence. Whoever disposes the right type of wisdom, capable of making children worthy of their people bequeathes them with such wisdom without constraint. And so the griots, the elders, professional story-tellers all take part in this august assignment. Senghor, despite his great European culture and education, still hears the voices of Elissa elders, or the lessons of Toke Waly, just as Dadié or Camara Laye hear the voices of their uncles. The intrusion of Western schools (with formal education) into rural Africa brought to a regrettable end this informal but invaluable pedagogic experience enjoyed by the child, thus prompting the Diallobe chief, in *Ambiguous Adventure*[8], to ask whether what African children learn in these schools is worth what they are obliged to give up and forget.

Samba Diallo's case illustrates another aspect of childhood, this time in Islamic regions of Africa while Senghor, Dadié or Camara Laye depict the frolicsome liberty of the African child in the more liberal, animist or Christian West Africa. Cheikh Hamidou Kane presents childhood in a world that 'believes in the end of the world', where no church bells are heard. Nonetheless, Samba Diallo's austere childhood complements that of Laye or Dadié, inasmuch as both of them aim at a more grandiose vision of human existence and nature. This vision would have been incomplete without the experiences in the French schools which, as it were, represented another type of truth and knowledge indispensable for the very emergence of a 'perfect' African in the face of colonial changes. This reverse of the coin, by its comparative and contrastive nature, gave greater depth to young African personalities that were to see themselves at the helm of affairs, charting a new political and social destiny for their peoples.

Although Western school experience for African children is represented in literature as a destabilizing factor in their lives, alienatory in nature and capable of creating such cultural ambiguities as Samba Diallo (incomplete metamorphosis, a nameless hybrid) or such 'revolte' as Medza in *Mission Terminée* (*Mission to Kala*)[9], it is generally seen as a survival strategy in a world where, in the words of the Grande Royale in *Ambiguous Adventure*, the time has come to teach African children to 'live', seeing that they too will have to deal with a new world society where archaic values and practices will be stultified and bankrupt. The exposure of children to these situations permits them to quietly, unobtrusively compose their personality in a sensibly harmonious combination of culture and education. Sooner or later however, they are made to feel that Western education could be liberating or ensnaring, enriching or insidiously harmful, depending on the prudence or imprudence of its African convert.

Certain aspects of African childhood, however, seem to need reappraisal. Respect for age, obedience to elders are good qualities; but total self-effacement and the requirement to live according to prescribed rules discourage initiative and the spirit of enquiry. Africans, therefore, in spite of their wealth of moral disposition appear much more intimidated and disarmed than their Western counterparts in the face of certain challenges. Besides, the informal nature of children's education which, among other things, discriminates between maleness and femaleness, appears to create gender chauvinism for the one and an inferiority complex (therefore a psychosocial handicap) for the other. This cultural inequality narrows education down for the female, with the sole aim of producing a decent woman capable of being a worthy wife to a man, whereas the male enjoys all the privileges that enable him to carry on with traditions and values of the family and clan. Childhood for the female is therefore one of diverse, severe constraints for,

> No matter how prosperous a man was,
> if he was unable to rule his women
> and children he was not really a man.[10]

Although the needs and sensibilities of children are considered a legitimate priority they lack the type of autonomy enjoyed by their Western European counterparts. But the apparent material penury of existence does not however symbolize a less fulfilling quality of life.

However, African childhood is not always absolute submission to parental will, or willingness to allow others to dispose of his life. Conflicts, sometimes complex in nature, do arise between father and daughter or son or more rarely between mother and daughter. Usually mother and daughter, being the oppressed gender, share secrets that the father is not privileged to know. Jupiter in his kingdom, the traditional African father, is a man to be feared. To call children to instant discipline it suffices to warn them that their father will be informed of their misdemeanour on his return. Fathers dispense instant and sometimes severe justice and it is not a pleasant experience for an offending child to consider what father will do on his return. Most fathers are taciturn and Nestor-faced at home in the presence of wife and children who tremble and fear his anger. After all, the child is only a 'drop of his liquid', and should therefore submit meekly to the father's little tyrannies.

When Toundi in *Une vie de boy* (*Houseboy*) rebelled against this continued ill-treatment he knew at once that the time had come to part ways with his father. Consequently his refuge in the mission and his subsequent employment as the Commandant's boy produced the rare and juicy episodes which make Ferdinand Oyono's novel the classic that it is today. Before Toundi, Achebe presented Nwoye, Okonkwo's son who, frustrated and mortified by the intimidatory parental authority of his 'roaring flame' of a father, chose to flee to the missionaries whom his father had vowed not to tolerate in Umuofia. Traditional Africa loves the male child and upholds that he is 'king', but he is king only so long as he dances to the whims and caprices of his father, the Zeus of the 'domus'. Some fathers are so intransigent as to appear as monsters in the eyes of their children. This is the case of Medza in *Mission to Kala*.

> My father ... twenty years of terror almost constant. In a moment, and at a place, I least expect him, he emerges, like a phantom, and immediately demands account of my behaviour; what I had done, where I went, whether I had worked studiously at school, whether my conduct was satisfactory, if I

would pass my exams . . . detective . . . worse than a detective, he was a home dictator, a house tyrant.
Never was there any peace, any security.[11]

This tyranny of many years soured the natural relationship between father and son, and gradually incubated the eventual revolt of the victim. Not only could Medza not do well at school, but the rancour against his father turned him into a tamer of the 'dragon' (p. 230), earning him the liberty and self possession that had eluded him for more than twenty years. The father–daughter conflict is dramatized when marriage is in question. Here the father exercises absolute authority totally disregarding the opinions of either wife or daughter. His criteria for a suitable husband include wealth, a good government post, influence etc., but exclude his daughter's love for a particular suitor. Kany, in Seydou Badian's *Sous l'orage*, may be in love, and wish ardently to marry the love of her life, but her father obstinately prefers his choice of a rich local farmer, with three or four wives and with whom Kany, an educated girl, is totally incompatible.

Childhood, like the past with which it is associated, occupies a prominent psychological part of African literature. The evocation of individual childhood, calls up as a corollary the evocation of Africa's 'childhood' itself, which, in effect, is an indirect apology and illustration of its splendour before the advent of colonization.

It is for this reason that the theme of childhood, far from being mere exoticism, symbolizes all the moral and natural nobleness that Africa ever stood for. Rediscovering this glory is in a way an indirect exhortation to the Africans engrossed in the pursuit of Westernization and its allurements, to retrace their steps back to the honourable values they are inclined to despise thus re-equipping themselves with the pride of their worth and the psychological reassurance vital to their existence and rejuvenation.

## NOTES

1. Bernard Dadié, *Climbié* (Paris: Seghers, 1956).
2. Léopold Sédar Senghor, *Liberté 3* (Paris: Seuil Edition, 1977).
3. Bernard Dadié, *Climbié*, trans. Karen Chapman (London: Heinemann, 1971).
4. Seydou Badian, *Sous l'orage* (Paris: Présence Africaine, 1973).
5. Léopold Sédar Senghor, 'Chaka' in *Poèmes* (Paris: Seuil Edition, 1964).
6. Mircea Eliade, *Mythes, rêves et mystères* (Paris: Gallimard, 1957) 45.
7. Senghor, *Poèmes* 15.
8. Cheikh Hamidou Kane, *Ambiguous Adventure* (Paris, Union Générale d'Editions, 1961) 44.
9. Mongo Beti, *Mission to Kala* (*Mission Terminée*) (Paris: Buchet/Chastel, 1957) 100–101.
10. Chinua Achebe, *Things Fall Apart* (London: Heinemann, 1976) 37.
11. Beti, 232.

## 'Beloved Pawns': The Childhood Experience in the Novels of Chinua Achebe & Mongo Beti

N. F. Inyama

In their criticism of African fiction, scholars and other commentators have been partial to the exposition of the 'public', as opposed to the 'private' themes of the novels. Such a critical preference has been based on what are probably considered as the more 'relevant' concerns of the various authors. For example, although the family and the dynamics of its relationships constitute powerful thematic under-currents in novels by Achebe, Armah, Ngugi, Beti, Munonye, Nwapa and others, much of the criticism of these authors' works focuses predominantly on such issues as the conflict of cultures, the colonial experience, post-colonial political dilemmas, public corruption, alienation, and technical aspects like language and narrative structure. Issues such as marital, parent – child, and kinship relationships and conflicts, as well as childhood experiences have either been totally ignored or have only been peripherally hinted at by critics concerned with more 'significant' issues.

Yet a substantial number of African novels are extensively dependent for the complexity of their plots and thematic success on the degree to which their authors have interwoven their public themes with the more intimate themes of family life and experience. As if in direct confirmation of Ruth N. Anshen's observation in *The Family: Its Functions and Destiny*, that the family is the primary source of all experience, both positive and negative, one finds that where tragedy or disillusionment feature in these novels, the authors have usually anchored such a consequence on some family-based mischance or experience. Also, the exploration of motive, as well as character development, is set against the background of the childhood experiences of the main protagonists and important minor characters.

Chinua Achebe and Mongo Beti are two novelists who explore the childhood experience in their works. Achebe does this principally in *Things Fall Apart* and *Anthills of the Savannah*, while Beti gives us images of childhood in *Mission to Kala*. Read from this particular perspective, one is left to draw the inescapable conclusion that for the characters concerned – Nwoye, Beatrice (BB), Jean Marie – childhood is an experience soured by extreme parental authority, that of the father, who is generally more concerned with the enhancement or projection of his own ego and image and victimizes the child in the pursuit of such an objective. Furthermore, the images of childhood presented in these two writers' works run almost directly counter to the warm, paradisical images recalled in Camara Laye's *The African Child*.

Achebe's *Things Fall Apart* is set in the patriarchal Igbo world of its hero, Okonkwo, who aspires to the achievement of the most cherished distinctions of this cultural environment. He is also determined to bury forever, through his own achievements, the memory of Unoka, his improvident, non-achieving father. Okonkwo pursues his ambition with passion and counts the milestones of his progress: wrestling champion, brave warrior, successful farmer and provider, husband of three wives, and father of many children. But even as he records these achievements, Okonkwo's 'whole life was dominated by fear, the fear of failure and of weakness . . . It was the fear of himself, lest he should be found to resemble his father' (pp. 10–11). Achebe tells us further that 'Okonkwo ruled his household with a heavy hand. His wives, especially the youngest, lived in perpetual fear of his fiery temper, and so did his little children' (p. 10).

In elaborating on this response by the children to their father's ways and nature, Achebe focuses mainly on Nwoye, Okonkwo's first son, but the reader is expected to deduce through this what childhood in Okonkwo's household would be like for the rest of the children. Okonkwo's cruelties to Nwoye are coloured by his own peculiar perception of the importance of the first son in Igbo family culture: the first son is seen as the most potent proof of a man's manhood and an assurance of family continuity. But in time with his partial perception of the significance of things in his culture, Okonkwo sees the upbringing of his son as an enterprise in the projection of his own self-image. Nwoye is denied the joy of a carefree childhood in a prosperous household by Okonkwo's 'constant nagging and beating. And so Nwoye was developing into a sad-faced youth' (p. 11). It would be difficult to imagine any of Okonkwo's children recalling childhood with affection or warmth, since the household is dominated by the fear of its ruler, and since, in any case, Okonkwo believed that the only emotion worth showing openly was that of anger. The limit of his parental affection is to regret both secretly and openly, that Ezinma, his lively daughter, was not born a boy.

Okonkwo's approach to child-rearing is aimed at the duplication of his own image and the enhancement of his own personality and reputation in his son. Thus he inflicts on the young boy an oppressive and manipulative regime that is unlikely to produce a well-grounded and well-balanced person for the community. Nwoye must resemble him. As he tells his friend, Obierika, shortly after he had killed Ikemefuna,

> But I can tell you, Obierika, my children do not resemble me. Where are the
> young suckers that will grow when the old banana tree dies? If Ezinma had
> been a boy I would have been happier. She has the right spirit. (pp. 57–8)

He dismisses Obierika's statement that 'the children are still very young' by claiming that 'Nwoye is old enough to impregnate a woman. At his age I was already fending for myself' (p. 58). Okonkwo wants Nwoye – and by extension all his children – to make quantum leaps from babyhood to adulthood or manhood without the intervening period of childhood.

One result of Okonkwo's approach to parenthood is to create in Nwoye a false, dissimulating childhood existence. To please Okonkwo and escape his 'constant nagging and beating' Nwoye spends his early boyhood pretending to be what he is not: a lover of Okonkwo's 'masculine stories of violence and bloodshed' (p. 47). But what Nwoye would have preferred to do at this stage in his life was to listen to 'the stories that his mother used to tell, and which she no doubt still told her younger children – stories of the tortoise and his wily ways, . . .' (p. 46).

> That was the kind of story that Nwoye loved. But he now knew that they were
> for foolish women and children and he knew that his father wanted him to be
> a man. And so he feigned that he no longer cared for women's stories. And
> when he did this he saw that his father was pleased, and no longer rebuked
> him or beat him. (pp. 46–7)

Nwoye's childhood is spent in this conflicting pull between the warm, magical world of fancy and imagination, represented by his mother's hut and the stories she tells, and Okonkwo's 'realistic' world of action and violence. Okonkwo makes a Gradgrindian effort to bleach the world of fancy out of his son, especially because it portends danger, as he believes, to the child's future as a strong man who could 'rule his women and children (and especially his women)' in his own style (p. 46). But in the process of bending Nwoye to his will, Okonkwo, as Alan Shelston says of Dickens's character, Murdstone, substitutes 'judicious fatherhood' with 'brutal firmness'.

As I stated earlier, Okonkwo's approach to fatherhood, with regard to Nwoye, is founded on a considerable level of selfishness. He would want to produce a clone of himself, so that in life, and even after death, his image and reputation would remain intact. Okonkwo's selfish goals embody a quality described as 'ego-narcissism' by Sven Armens in his *Archetypes of the Family in Literature* – a self-adulating and self-projecting quality which in its extreme form sacrifices natural parental affection for artificial selfish goals. In Armens's view, this characteristic is pre-eminently manifested in the Greek legend of Agamemnon's abjuring parental affection and sacrificing his own daughter in the interest of the state and his own reputation or image as a leading patriot.

In *Things Fall Apart* Okonkwo fulfills this archetypal image: in obedience to the dictates of the state and protection of his reputation as a strong man of action, he jettisons parental affection and cuts down Ikemefuna who calls him 'father'. The significant point being made is that in the pursuit of his self-glorifying goals, Okonkwo ruins Nwoye's childhood for him, using his 'brutal firmness' to purge it of happiness, and climaxing this warped approach to fatherhood with the destruction of the boy's childhood friend, Ikemefuna. One ultimate cumulative result of Nwoye's unhappy childhood is the outright rejection of the father who had made his childhood such a long misery, as well as the rejection of the culture which seemed to sanction this process.

In *Arrow of God* Achebe briefly hints at the continuation of his investigation of manipulative fatherhood and its effects on the childhood experiences of his characters. The reader gets sharp glimpses of the conflicts that exist in Ezeulu's relationships with his sons. These conflicts are paralleled and amplified in the more complex and conflict-ridden relationship existing between Ezeulu and the larger Umuaro community. He would prefer them to see and interpret events from his perspective, a perspective sanctioned and even sanctified by his own priestly insights. Rarely does he get this co-operation from some members of the clan, led in their opposition by Nwaka of Umuneora, and Ezeidemili, the priest of Idemili, who resent what they see as Ezeulu's overbearing and scheming ways.

Within his own household, Ezeulu expects the same kind of total obedience from his sons, as well as an unquestioning trust in his wisdom. Although he lacks the harsh brutality of Okonkwo, the limit of his fatherly affection is determined by the degree to which each son lives up to this child-like submission to him. In other words, this affection is effectively truncated for each child as soon as he begins to show an independent response to the world around him.

Edogo, his oldest son, observes that Ezeulu

> must go on treating his grown children like little boys, and if they said no there was a big quarrel. This was why the older his children grew the more he seemed to dislike them. Edogo remembered how much his father had liked him when he was a boy and how with the passage of years he had transferred his affection first to Obika and then to Oduche and Nwofo. (p. 113)

In childhood, therefore, the experience of affection in this father-focused family culture is a rather brief affair, the loss of which breeds and fuels a long-lingering resentment, produces frequent arguments between father and children, and generates thinly-veiled disloyalty. At some point or other, Ezeulu's self-enhancing efforts to manipulate his sons' childhoods towards an absolute trust in him and his views collapse, and this collapse promptly diminishes his affection for them.

Achebe returns to the theme of childhood in greater detail in *Anthills of the Savannah*, through the recollections of childhood memories by its heroine, Beatrice (BB). In spite of this character being a woman, the recollection of the childhood experience shares a similarity with *Things Fall Apart* and *Arrow of God* in being father-focused.

BB's recollections give the reader a strong impression of a family world that is far from affectionate. For her, particularly, this family environment had nursed a special resentment for her being yet a fifth girl in a household that was in desperate need of a male child – hence the middle name she hates, 'Nwanyibuife: A woman is also something', or Buife, for short. Her father, in his mission-teacher approach to family discipline, flogs his children at the slightest provocation. Although some of the details of these recollections might be erroneous – the suspicion that .her mother was also flogged by her father, for instance – yet she effectively presents images of a grim childhood world, a childhood of aloneness in an otherwise well peopled household:

> Throughout my life I have never sought attention; not even as a child. I can see, looking back at my earliest memories, a little girl completely wrapped up in her own little world – a world contained, like Russian dolls, inside the close-fitting world of our mission house . . . . (p. 84)

> He was a very stern man, my father – as distant from us children as from our poor mother. As I grew older I got to know that his whip was famous not only in our house and in the schoolhouse next door but throughout the diocese. (p. 85)

> There were times I suspected he may have flogged our poor mother, though . . . I never actually saw it happen. None of my sisters had seen it either, or if they did they preferred not to tell me, for they never took me much into confidence. Looking back on it I am sometimes amazed at the near-conspiracy in which they circled me most of the time. . . . it [the suspected flogging] didn't happen too often, though. But it always made me want to become a sorceress that could say '*Die!*' to my father and he would die as in the folktale. And then, when he had learnt his lesson, I would bring him back to life and he would never touch his whip again. . . .
> I couldn't have been more than seven or eight years old at the time but I know I had this strong feeling – extraordinary, powerful, adult – that my father and my mother had their own world, my three sisters had theirs and I was alone in mine. And it didn't bother me at all then, my aloneness, nor has it done so since. . . .
> I didn't realise until much later that my mother bore me a huge grudge because I was a girl – her fifth in a row though one had died – and that when I was born she had so desperately prayed for a boy to give my father. (pp. 86–7)

Although BB asserts that her aloneness never bothered her, the reader can easily pierce through this claim to detect the underlying unhappiness. Indeed, the fact that she can recall these childhood images with such vivid and grim succinctness after so many years confirms the suspicion of their powerful impact on her psyche. Her childhood world was one in which her attempt at affectionate solidarity with her victimized mother was rewarded with a violent push that landed her head against a wooden mortar, a world whose lack of fatherly affection was further symbolized by the sharp spanking, rather than consolation, which her father gave her when she fell off a mango tree. Again, in Achebe's handling, the father is the primary focus of the childhood consciousness in this story: he is strict, unaffectionate, and colours the childhood world in cheerless hues. Furthermore, the heroine's seeming indifference to her aloneness is a rejection of the world which had held sad memories for her.

In *Mission to Kala* Mongo Beti paints various ironic images of the colonial enterprise and those at the receiving end. These are transmitted through the experiences of the novel's hero, Jean Marie Medza. By the time his rescue mission is over, Jean Marie has been transformed in many different ways – he has become a man, in fact.

One of the most striking aspects of this novel, however, is that it ends on a final encounter between the hero and his father. In recounting this event – his final liberation from oppressive fatherhood – Jean Marie gives the reader a detailed picture of his family world and childhood memories. Once again, the father is the primary figure, the shadow that darkens this environment. As he rides back from his mission, Jean Marie looks ahead to the impending, explosive encounter with his father and, as it were, builds his case against the man:

> My father: the words evoked twenty years of almost continued terror. . . . He was like a bloody policeman – no, worse: a private dictator, a domestic tyrant. There was never any peace or sense of security; nothing but rows, reproaches and fear.
>
> He had packed me off to school as young as he could. My mother had been unwise enough to protest, and this had earned her a formidable dressing down, poor dear. She said no more, simply formed a silent opposition. My father had been obsessively determined that I should get immediate promotion from one class to the next every term without ever staying put any longer. There were endless private confabulations with the masters. 'Please,' he would say, 'punish him as often as he deserves it. Do not be swayed by any regard for my feelings.' (p. 164)

There is deliberate irony in the last statement, for Jean Marie has already convinced his readers, or at least has tried to persuade them, to see the older Medza as anything but affectionate, and that he would feel almost nothing if anything unfortunate befell the boy. Jean Marie presses this image of an unfriendly father, one who does not even give him an education out of altruism, but for other remote and vindictive reasons. He counts the cost of this 'educational' process, which he and others of his generation were forced to suffer through: it is a painful elegy to a lost childhood:

> Do you remember that period? Fathers used to take their children to school as they might lead sheep into a slaughterhouse. Tiny tots, would turn from backwood villages thirty or forty miles up-country, shepherded by their parents, to be put on the books of some school, it didn't matter which. They formed a miserable floating population, these kids: lodged with distant relations who happened to live near the school, underfed, scrawny, bullied all day by ignorant monitors. The books in front of them presented a universe which had nothing in common with the one they knew: they battled endlessly with the unknown, astonished and desperate and terrified. We were those children – it is not easy to forget – and it was our parents who forced this torment on us. Why did they do it? (p. 165)

For the hero, the outside childhood world of school, grimly frightening as it is, is only a replication of a joyless family world:

> My father scolded everyone, and my mother scolded the children – all except the eldest, and there was a good reason for this exception: the boy was hardly ever at home. When he did turn up, there was no question of being cross with him, one harsh word and he would vanish again. When it came to the children themselves, the boys took it out on the girls, and the elder sister told off the younger. . . . Everyone scolded and thrashed everyone else, everyone had their preordained victim; and it was the head of the household who set the example that they followed. (pp. 169–70)

Certain conclusions may be drawn from the works of the two authors examined in the foregoing paragraphs. Firstly, the childhood experiences they record run directly counter to what we perceive in Camara Laye's *The African Child*, in their grim unhappiness. Secondly, the primary, almost exclusive focuses of these recollections of childhood experiences are on the father of the family; this is perhaps made inevitable by the patriarchal environments of the novels' settings. Finally, the cumulative result of these experiences for the characters involved is the rejection of these childhood worlds. Nwoye rejects Okonkwo and his community's values. BB's aloneness alienates her from her parents and sisters, and Jean Marie more or less concludes his tale with these words:

> I have never returned home – and, indeed, never shall till after my father's death, and only then to comfort my poor mother. (p. 182)

Medza's inconsistencies and unreliability as a narrator have been remarked upon by previous critics, but despite all that, there is a convincing ring to his words when he talks about his childhood experiences near his father.

# WORKS CITED

Achebe, Chinua. *Things Fall Apart*. London: Heinemann, 1958.
——. *Arrow of God*. London: Heinemann, 1964.
——. *Anthills of the Savannah*. Ibadan: Heinemann, 1988.
Anshen, Ruth Nanda, ed. *The Family: Its Function and Destiny*. New York: Harper & Row, 1959.
Armens, Sven Magnus. *Archetypes of the Family in Literature*. Seattle and London: University of Washington Press, 1966.
Beti Mongo. *Mission to Kala*, Trans. Peter Green. London: Heinemann, 1964.
Laye, Camara. *The African Child*, Trans. James Kirkup. Glasgow: William Collins, 1959.
Shelston, Alan. 'Past and Present in *David Copperfield*.' *Critical Quarterly* 27.3 (Autumn, 1985): 17–33.

# The Symbolic Concept of Childhood in Chukwuemeka Ike's *The Potter's Wheel* & *The Bottled Leopard*

## Ezenwa-Ohaeto

The depiction of childhood in modern African fiction has taken varied forms. The portrayals range from Chinua Achebe's use of children to reflect linguistic variation, Wole Soyinka's metaphoric exploration of childhood in his autobiography, to Camara Laye's nostalgic but didactic analysis of childhood.

Among Nigerian novelists, Chukwuemeka Ike has not only presented realistic portraits of childhood but has also proceeded to symbolize its concept in novels constructed out of a variety of myths, legends, fictions, cultural notions and colonial and modernistic influences. The novelist clearly proceeds beyond the observation that 'a didactic or moral stance has always been part of his culture's literature for juveniles' (Osa, 1987: 9), to widen the concept of childhood and subject it to symbolic interpretations. This quality does not detract from the realism of the fiction because even at the surface level, the stories are captivating enough to arouse an interesting literary appreciation.

*The Potter's Wheel* derives its dynamic narrative qualities from the activities of the major protagonist thus confirming the view that

> the desire to create characters and reproduce them in such a manner that the social and human motives that led them to certain actions are felt, is demonstrated through the artistic device of characterization in the novels of Chukwuemeka Ike. (Ezenwa-Ohaeto, 1991: 125)

The emphatic stress on the major character is conveyed through an authorial comment that 'Obuechina was the only boy out of seven children born to Mazi Lazarus Maduabuchi and his wife' (p. 9). His unique status is reflected in the fact that although she has six other children she is referred to as 'Mama Obu as if she had no other children' (p. 10). His father takes the unpopular decision to send him to the home of a teacher and his childless wife as a ward. The author uses this decision to symbolize the necessity for supervising childhood because Mazi Lazarus is neither indigent nor handicapped but he is aware of the limitations of doting parents in the effective training of children.

However, the endemic quality of Obuechina (Obu) is his fascinating brilliance which belies his unflattering physical appearance of a large head, diminutive nose and thin body.

Chukwuemeka Ike presents Obu at various stages of his childhood through contrasts in order to illustrate the two aspects of positive and negative manifestations in life. Samuel the bully who oppresses Obu and Oti epitomizes this negative dimension and Obu recollects at one point

> all the tricks Samuel played on them including making them bruise their knuckles by goading them into a silly contest to determine whose knuckles would produce the loudest noise when knocked against the stonehard tip of an old pair of shoes . . . . Afraid to offend him, they would go on knocking at the shoe until one of them, unable to bear further bruises, burst into tears. (p. 16)

Samuel's behaviour symbolizes children who are not refined by effective parental guidance as Mama Obu tells Samuel's mother: 'People say you are responsible for his actions. You heap sand around his waist, you prop him up in his vicious action' (p. 21). The irony is that Mama Obu equally culpably spoils her son who 'shared her bed with her' and she 'kept his supper handy so that he could have it at whatever time of night he called for it' (p. 25). The behaviour of both mothers symbolizes the debilitating influence of parents who over-protect their children thus, the author implies, inadvertently turning them into social deviants.

The novelist writes approvingly of children who exhibit leadership qualities as when David transforms one of the children's masquerades at Umuchukwu into an impressive affair with songs and fascinating masquerade costumes: 'David's experience outside Umuchukwu marked him out as leader of his age-group. His expertise in turning out a masquerade further strengthened his claims' (p. 27). The accomplishments of David are part of what Mazi Lazarus, Obu's father, expects from his own son because 'all he wanted was to establish the principle that every person who breathes must regard work as an essential ingredient of life, and everybody who eats food must work for it' (p. 28). It is to ensure that Obu learns the rewards of hard work that his father sends him to live with a teacher and his wife. In line with the view that the

> philosophy underlying the upbringing of children in traditional African societies [stresses that] hardship and suffering, far from causing psychological damage to the young child, strengthens him and prepares him for the tasks ahead. (Ugbabe, 1988: 69)

Mazi Lazarus' perturbation is not mistaken because his son is 'slowly but surely developing into a useless boy. He took no part in anything that was done in the house; all he wanted was to be left to wake up at his leisure, to be given what food he wanted at any time he wanted it, and to be free to play whenever he was not eating or sleeping' . . . (p. 58). Such deficiencies clearly constitute major flaws in the development of any child in the society in which Obu and his father live. In effect Ike is portraying not only those constituent elements of character formulation peculiar to that society but also the values in a wider context of human relationships.

This wider fictive context of *The Potter's Wheel* becomes apparent as Obu is sent to live with a teacher and his wife at Aka. The symbolic dimensions of the novel also assume interesting features through the presentation of Teacher Zacheus as a dwarfish 'dare-devil who carried out his intentions without caring whose ox was gored'; who 'also carried a *Koboko*, a long leather whip, which he administered to any pedestrian who got in the way of his bicycle' (p. 68) and Madam Deborah his wife who 'at the age of only six showed that even at that tender age her granite heart had become clearly evident' (p. 69). This teacher and his wife are the visible spheres of authority in total control of the boys and girls in their domain. Obu discovers that in his new environment, he has to develop strategies for survival. This discovery is made under unpleasant circumstances because in his first encounter with the boy Silence, another servant in the house, he 'felt that all he had to do was to recount his unpleasant experience and everyone would exonerate him and condemn Silence. To his utter consternation, both judge and jury found him guilty on both counts' (p. 100). Obu, therefore, not only learns a new set of rules among the servants but also how to cope with his guardians in a constant battle of wits. Thus when he spoils the yam pottage by adding too much salt and Madam gives 'him the knock-out smack which was believed in Umuchukwu to turn the recipient into a grass cutter' (p. 108) he does not even 'shed a tear' and wonders if he 'was already developing a houseboy's crocodile skin' (p. 109).

The transformation of Obu is clearly symbolic and it owes its dynamics to the other servants. Silence teaches him the art of pretence like his deliberate show of haste when he 'almost pushed Obu and Mary down in an effort to demonstrate how seriously he took his charge' (p. 113). This is why later in the novel the author informs us that

> Obu was learning the ropes. The ability to hoodwink Teacher or Madam constituted the greatest asset of any servant finding himself in their service. The spontaneity with which he had told a plausible lie, the dexterity with which he had conveyed a Kernel past Madam's observatory indicated that he was picking up fast from his more experienced comrades. (p. 134)

However, Madam still astounds the servants with her uncanny ability to spot their tricks and they believe that she must be a witch because 'only a witch could read their minds or eavesdrop on their conversation that way. It was pointless trying to trick a witch' (p. 139). This uncanny ability is shared by Teacher especially when he detected Obu's forgery of a letter purporting to come from his mother. He secretly admired the boy's cleverness: 'I did not flog him as I should. I like to recognize cleverness when I see it' (p. 144). This cleverness is clearly what the novelist is interested in illustrating symbolically as an element that is capable of either aiding the development of the child or destroying it. Obviously Madam and Teacher are only applying adult intelligence to the activities of children to the astonishment of the latter. Perhaps this is what Wilson-Tagoe has in mind when she insists that 'the world of childhood is in so many senses, a separate and different world, often free from the system of alliances that colour and constrain human relationships in the adult world' (Wilson-Tagoe, 1992: 19). It is clearly the tension between these two worlds – the adult's and the child's – that Ike consistently interrogates in the novel and whose symbolic implications he projects in terms of the interests, responses and feelings of the characters.

Nevertheless it is interesting that Teacher trains his servants to be wily for he sends Silence ostensibly to buy beer but with a secret signal that he should not buy anything. Silence dutifully complies and returns with an appropriate story: 'they say the man who sells beer for Dinah has been conscripted into the army, and she has not found another person to take his place. The shop is locked, and there is nobody to open it for me' (p. 155). But Teacher is not training the children to become dishonest adults because he disgraces Obu publicly when he steals meat from the soup pot. In effect Teacher is emphasizing that cleverness must be situated on a foundation of valid morals and this attitude appears to incorporate the symbolic presentation of cleverness in the novel. In addition, the morality of the girls is supervised by Madam who, for instance, watches Mary closely so that she does not fall prey to some of the unscrupulous men in her vicinity. Thus childhood in *The Potter's Wheel* is associated with a moral consciousness through its symbolic concept.

Furthermore the victories of the children in their conflicts with Teacher and Madam and the wider society are symbolic. One such is Ada's psychological victory over Madam when she accepts her undeserved punishment without flinching: 'she emerged from the whole incident with a feeling of liberation. Madam never again attempted to strike her' (p. 159). But there are the major victories in the wider society involving the vicarious participation of the adults. When Silence wins the quarter-mile race, for instance, he receives 'a congratulatory smile from Madam and a promise of another pair of shorts from Teacher' (p. 174). In addition he is feted by the whole school and similarly Nmagwu, the female champion of the school, is 'carried shoulder high by her school mates as they danced to the music of their brass band'

(p. 178). The portrayal of the two champions as male and female illustrates symbolically the author's concept of childhood as essential in the provision of unfettered routes of progress for both male and female children.

However, Chukwuemeka Ike's portrayal of inter-gender relationships among children indicates that they could be destroyed when they are coloured by the alliances or prejudices of adults. The author asserts the necessity for amity through the relationship between Margaret and Obu. She gives him presents of 'Giant ukwa, fried without being burnt and nicely shelled ready for the mouth', (p. 126) while he reciprocates with gifts of roast termites. This relationship progresses naturally and pleasantly until the intrusion of the adult Monday, who intimidates Obu with the prospect that he will become an 'Osu' (a cultural outcast) if he continues to associate with Margaret. This false statement is merely to frighten the boy into concealing his discovery of Monday and a girl making love in the bush. This is a symbolic demonstration that quite often the severance of relationships and the generation of hatred are the results of selfish interests.

In Umuchukwu Obu is a privileged son but in Aka he is a despised servant subjected to all the deprivations of such situations. Thus, Obu's dreams of Aka that occur in the midst of the pleasures of Umuchukwu juxtapose to his dreams of Umuchukwu that occur in the midst of the suffering at Aka symbolize the author's concept of childhood as a parallel to life which possesses alternate experiences of pain and joy. These dreams also emphasize the subtle changes taking place in the boy and the positive effects of those changes as expressed by Mazi Lazarus: 'Missus don't you see what change Oniyibo (Obu) has undergone? Do you see how he has been going on errands cheerfully? Did you notice that nobody told him to join his sisters in carrying yams this morning, and yet he joined them happily?' (p. 210). This implies that childhood offers enough indicators of the image of the future adult which is obviously part of Chukwuemeka Ike's considered view of the importance of childhood.

The symbolic portrayal of childhood continues in *The Bottled Leopard*, set in a secondary school. Some of the children in this novel are slightly older than those in *The Potter's Wheel* but 'some characters can also be called "children" although they are physically and even psychologically adults' (Naumann, 1992: 36). In addition the parental influence is slightly diminished because the children reside in the school. Ike, however, expands the focus of this novel to incorporate not only the academic activities of the children but also the cultural norms and mores associated with their individual traditions. The novel is constructed around Ugochukwu Amobi who gains admission into the prestigious Government College for further education.

Quite early in the novel, the author interrogates the issue of education as a protagonist wonders about 'a school where you could earn a sentence of two hours detention, with hard labour, for speaking your own language . . . It must be English morning, afternoon, evening and night. Presumably you must dream in English too!' (p. 11). This interrogation is at the centre of the novel's concept of childhood because the author demonstrates through the story the effects, consequences and implications of the aim of the institution in 'transforming young African youth into English gentlemen (p. 12). But the irony which materializes is that both the staff and students are caught in a situation where they unconsciously indicate that the influence and power of their mythological traditions colour their thoughts and views, and this dilemma is particularly prominent among the children.

Ike builds the story gradually before this interrogation of education and its ostensible profits for the child, through the activities of his characters. The presentation of the adventure of Amobi and Chuk in the school orchard is used to emphasize the constant tension between the excitement of the imagination of children on the one hand and the essential but often problematic insistence that they conform to the standards of the society on the other. The thoughts of Amobi reflect this tension as he ruminates: 'How on earth could the Principal develop such a mouth-watering orchard and expect a dwarf wall, a man-made gate, and an unarmed elderly and arthritic watchman to keep vivacious, adventurous students away from its pleasures?' (p. 15). Thus the decision of Amobi and Chuk the mulatto boy, to go to the orchard at night; an adventure that is usually embarked on by the students at one time or the other becomes a symbol of childhood exuberance that must be controlled in order to prevent it from degenerating into negative traits.

The author also juxtaposes the image of the child as a symbol of hope in the new dispensation of education with the image of the child as an inheritor of a vibrant tradition of folk wisdom that survives from the old dispensation. One instance of this juxtaposition is the manner in which Ike portrays Mazi Ezeanya and his wife, the parents of Amobi, who think that the eclipse of the sun portends doom and the way he shows Amobi providing the scientific explanation of the phenomenon to them: the 'Principal had given them advance notice of the eclipse, and Amobi had at once rushed off a letter home to warn his parents' . . . (p. 40). This constant tension between traditional beliefs and the modern concepts of reality is projected through Amobi's childhood experiences that are certainly symbolic.

In the mind of this child protagonist there is a constant play of doubts, hopes and notions. Amobi is also plagued by several questions in the church, the class and in the dormitory. He attends a Sunday service in which the story of a man possessed by a demon and how Jesus Christ transferred the evil spirits from him into swine, sparks off his inquisitive mind: 'he had re-read the passage twice immediately after the end of the service, as soon as he returned to his dormitory. And each time, he had seen a relationship between the story and the claims at home about men possessing leopards' (p. 54). However, his desire to expose these nagging doubts to the lens of the modern scientific thoughts available in the institution does not attract the relevant response – a reflection of both the impatience and ignorance of adults towards a child's normal attempts to unravel reality. This reaction appears to contradict the assertion that 'when a society is made up of isolated and segregated components that have been taught to look down upon their own cultural origins, having a common history, a common schooling and religion, should create a new cultural unity' (Pousse, 1992: 55). The common schooling at the Government College fails in this instance to obliterate the doubts of Amobi.

However, the cultural symbol created through the society portrayed in this novel is that childhood is not berefit of any of the lofty ideals and ideas associated with adults. In the school, for instance, the perennial issue of oppression in the society is microscoped through the activities of the Form Two bullies who force Chuk to drink a glass of urine labelled 'Formula Two', in order 'to put the bloated fag in his proper place' (p. 9). In addition, the incident involving Amobi and Daramola reflects this same microscopic presentation of the flaws in the wider society through children. Amobi narrates his unfortunate experience to Prefect Olatunji:

> I found my comb in pieces on my bed. One boy told me that he saw Daramola throw the broken pieces on my bed . . . I showed them to Daramola and asked him what I had done to him that he should break my comb like that. At first he pretended not to know what I was talking about, and ordered me to clear out . . . Instead of begging me for forgiveness, please, he put his hands on his hips like this, and asked me whether I knew he was a senior boy. He said that I should be happy that a senior boy broke my comb and ordered me to make myself scarce or he would shatter my jaw. (pp. 61–2)

The arrogance exhibited by Daramola is clearly utilized by the author to indicate symbolically through children, how adults in the wider society oppress and appropriate the resources of the weak. But it is not surprising that when such attitudes flourish even arbiters of justice such as the Prefects in the Government College misuse their powers.

Although the zealous manner in which Prefect Hammer maintains authority in the implementation of rules and regulations is commendable the author uses him to conceptualize the corruption of power at that level of childhood: 'as the College Prefect on duty, he was the visible symbol of authority, the Lord of all he surveyed. Until he said the grace, the meal could not start. And until he declared the meal over, you dared not leave your seat. If he declared you late, that meant no meal for you, no matter how hungry you might be' (p. 67). But

Prefect Hammer is also guilty of attempted homosexual rape as he 'drew Chuk closer, and held him tight breathing loudly' (p. 66). Chuk breaks free and runs away symbolizing that perversion can only occur when an unwilling individual fails to act decisively.

Within this concept of childhood and through the microscopic society inhabited by these children, Chukwuemeka Ike provides instances of positive influences and burgeoning positive moral consciousness. Kalu declares that he is 'Government Chemist-to-be' (p. 86) and this ambition spurs him to work hard. Similarly Akpan farms in order to procure money for his fees and as Kalu informs us even during holidays, 'he has to stay back to work in order to find money' (p. 90). In effect, Ike conceives childhood as a period when diverse influences impinge on the child but that each child is capable of either withstanding or succumbing to the negative influences, and this picture is symbolic of the adult society with its array of virtues and vices. The suspension of Amobi and Chuk for two weeks because they 'had sneaked out of their dormitory long after lights out to steal fruits' (p. 98), is an illustration of their inability to bridle their sense of adventure and curtail its negative influences which earns them the author's indictment and the Principal's condemnation. Although Mr Meniru, a staff member, consoles Amobi by saying that 'everyone thought of him as an admirable boy with a very bright potential', and although Chuk 'had something positive to contribute to the evolution of the College atmosphere and values' (p. 105), the author by their punishment, makes the point that in any sane society rules are fashioned for the establishment of justice and fair play and the inculcation of moral values.

Through Amobi's visit to his hometown during his suspension in the company of Chuk another aspect of Ike's symbolic concept of childhood is brought out. Coincidentally Amobi's childhood friend Nma, also returns home as a result of some mysterious occurrences. Ike uses Amobi and Nma through their individual but mysterious experiences symbolically to interrogate the prevalent notions associated with the traditional society especially among the educated. Interestingly the link between Amobi and Nma is not only in terms of these unsolicited encounters with supernatural powers but also in terms of academic activities. In the primary school, 'Nma had usually beaten him to second place in English language and Scripture but conceded first place to him on the aggregate, often with a slim margin' (p. 76). Ike clearly shows that success in life is not restricted by gender through his portrayal of Nma even as the relationship between the boy and the girl blossoms into love as they enter secondary school and she writes him a letter thus: 'Nkem, I am happy you like that blue handkerchief I made for you' (p. 70). Furthermore, their respective experience of the mysteries of their tradition brings them closer. In the girl's case it is diagnosed that 'a dead child was responsible for Nma's mysterious headache, her ultimate aim being to transfer her epilepsy to Nma' (p. 115), while Amobi is diagnosed to have inherited the leopard powers of his late Uncle Nnanyelugo. The events that lead to this discovery spawn further complications for Amobi at the Government College as a result of the harassment of a thief dressed like a leopard. Although Dibia Offia mysteriously but successfully 'bottles' – (literally cremates) the leopard powers of Amobi, this development does not prevent him from experiencing ostracism when Chuk who is aware of his powers, relates the story to the rest of the students. The painful aspect of this development is that Amobi, who had decided to take Chuk into confidence, is betrayed although 'Chuk had given his word' (p. 156). The subsequent exoneration of Amobi as the leopard thief when the thief Benjamin is caught and the eventual public apology from Chuk is contrived to illustrate how the flaws and frailties of adults could be discerned through the depiction of childhood.

The Principal puts it squarely when he admonishes Chuk who originates the claim that his classmate Amobi 'transformed himself into a live leopard whenever he desired'. The Principal further warns: 'Yet you peddled this allegation, thereby doing untold harm to an innocent boy who soon became associated with the so-called leopard harassing everyone here in recent weeks. Are you now convinced that you have borne false witness against your neighbour?' (p. 164). Although the students and staff members of the College are drawn into the wrong conclusion that leopard powers are non-existent, the author demonstrates through this symbolic concept of a childhood experience that betrayal of confidence and false allegations should be abhorred.

However, it is possible to read *The Bottled Leopard* as a childhood allegory in which the character symbolizes a people at a particular moment in their history. Amobi and Nma embody the hopes of their people and they also represent the struggle to construct a sense of stability out of the chaos of modernism. The *topos* of leopards and spirits of the dead people stand for the impediments that emanate from the tension between social forces and the traditional beliefs of the people. But in spite of this allegorical reading it is still possible to observe with Jacqueline Bardolph that 'the first stage, the early years in an autobiography' or a childhood novel 'brings to the reader the pleasure of recognizing his own childhood in any childhood' (Bardolph, 1992: 47). But the closing chapters of *The Bottled Leopard* indicates a loss of narrative intensity that could be seen as a petering out of inspiration. Nevertheless, through these child protagonists in *The Bottled Leopard* and *The Potter's Wheel* we find a symbolic concept of childhood dealing with a recovery of past memories and its rich webs of imaginary life, creativity, joys, pain, hopes and despair that project into the world of adults. Ike is clearly one of those writers identified elsewhere as capable of delving 'into the inner recess of the minds of children thereby exploring their actions through psychology and with both sympathy and artistic detachment' (Ezenwa-Ohaeto, 1992: 95).

The symbolic concept of childhood in *The Bottled Leopard* and *The Potter's Wheel* recreates movements from a childhood vision of life to an adult stage of maturity. It is also a movement from illusions to realities associated with the limits of human actions. The author does not construct childhood as a refuge of memory because the protagonists are not blind to the realities of adult life although their perceptions of those realities are pregnant with connotations and denotations. Chukwuemeka Ike's construction of children's apprehension of the world symbolizes an author's artistic way of suggesting the routes towards a refinement of social and cultural values.

---

## WORKS CITED

Bardolph, Jaqueline. 'Azaro, Saleem and Askar: brothers in allegory', *Commonwealth* 15.1 (Autumn 1992): 45–51.

Cuddon, J. A. 'Children's Books', *A Dictionary of Literary Terms*. London: Andre Deutsch, 1979 edn. 113–117.

Ezenwa-Ohaeto. 'The historical dimension of Chukwuemeka Ike's female characters', in Chidi Ikonne, Emelia Oko and Peter Onwudinjo, eds, *African Literature and African Historical Experiences*. Ibadan: Heinemann, 1991, 125–32.

—— 'Children, characterization and the didactic aspects of Nigerian children's fiction', in Chidi Ikonne, Emelia Oko and Peter Onwudinjo, eds, *Children and Literature in Africa*. Ibadan: Heinemann, 1992, 88–95.

Ike, Chukwuemeka. *The Potter's Wheel*. London: Fontana/Collins, 1973.

—— *The Bottled Leopard*. Ibadan: University Press, 1985.

Naumann, Michel. 'Coetzee's children of the earth and language', *Commonwealth* 15.1 (Autumn 1992): 36–8.

Osa, Osayimwense. *Nigerian Youth Literature*. Benin City: Paramount Publishers, 1987.

Pousse, Michel. 'The chaotic world of children in Lamming's *In the Castle of My Skin* and Naipaul's *The Mimic Men*', *Commonwealth* 15.1 (Autumn 1992): 52–60.

Ugbabe, Kanchana. 'The child figure in Chukwuemeka Ike's *The Potter's Wheel*', *Okike* 27/28 (1988): 67–73.

Wilson-Tagoe, Nana. 'Children's literature in Africa: theoretical and critical issues', in Chidi Ikonne, Amelia Oko and Peter Onwudinjo, eds, *Children and Literature in Africa*. Ibadan: Heinemann, 1992, 18–23.

---

## Aspects of Language in the African Literary Autobiography

---

Tony E. Afejuku

By 'literary autobiography' I mean an autobiographical narrative in which the autobiographer consciously or deliberately utilizes the resources of fiction, most especially a highly literary language, to transform his or her facts and reality into something else. The autobiographies by some of the 'accomplished masters of African prose fiction' (Traore, 1988: vii) which I am going to examine here and which fit this definition include the Guinean Camara Laye's *The African Child*, the Nigerian Wole Soyinka's *Aké; The Years of Childhood*, the Kenyan R. Mugo Gatheru's *Child of Two Worlds*, the South African Ezekiel Mphahlele's *Down Second Avenue* and Peter Abrahams's *Tell Freedom*. The rich texture of language of these autobiographies, apart from underscoring their artistry and aesthetic value, reminds us of Ezra Pound who succinctly said that 'Good writers are those who keep the language efficient. That is to say, keep it accurate, keep it clear' (p. 60). All the autobiographers here in varying degrees make use of language in this way, and part of their artistic success can be seen in this light. Specifically, I am going to focus on the writers' use of poetic language, dialogue, simple and complex language and their aesthetic effect on the autobiographies. These aspects of language will be examined from the point of view of the way autobiographers employ them to re-create setting – that is, atmosphere, mood, specific scenes and situations – and enrich their descriptions and narratives generally as literary re-creations.[1]

### Poeticization of setting

An element common to African literary autobiographies is that the authors enhance the aesthetic appeal of their works by poeticizing setting. They do this by employing lyrical evocations and also by making use of sound and rhythmic devices which bring to the reader sensuous gratification. For instance, in *Aké*, 'Soyinka pre-eminently shows himself as a boy discovering and himself as a man, through exercise of memory, discovering' (Olney, 1983:84) the enchanting life and landscape he and his fellow Aké inhabitants had always known. Although the landscape is gone in external reality: 'An evil thing has happened to Aké personage. The land is eroded, the lawns are bared and mystery driven from its once secretive comb' (*Aké*, p. 3), it is still vitally present in the sensibility of the artist that recalls it. This accounts for the lyrical – and hence fictional – re-creation of the smells, sounds, taste and sights of Aké:[2]

> The flavours of the market rose fully in the evenings beckoning us . . . For there they all were, together, the *jogi* seller who passed, in full lyrical cry beneath the backyard wall at a regular hour of the morning, followed only moments later by the *akara* seller, her fried bean-cakes still surreptitiously oozing and perfuming the air with groundnut oil. In the market we stood and gazed on the deftly cupped fingers of the old women . . . scooping out the white bean-paste from a mortar in carefully gauged quantities, into the wide-rimmed, shallow pots of frying oil . . . . Even when the *akara* was fried without any frills, its oil impregnated flavours filled the markets and jostled for attention with the tang of roasting coconut slices within farina cakes which we called *kasada*; with the hard-fried bean meat of *tinko*; the 'high', rotted-cheese smell of *ogiri*; roasting corn, fresh vegetables or *gbegiri*. *Akàmu*, the evening corn pap, was scooped into waiting bowls . . . by women who daily improvised new praise-chants. An *onini*, even a half-penny did not fulfil every craving but the sights and the smells were free. (pp. 153–4)

The aesthetic appeal of the above passage lies, among other things, in the systematically long sentences which parade a list of indigenous food items like jogi, akara, ogiri, kasada, tinko and akàmu. The systematically long sentences give the passage a special rhythm which helps to create a slow-motion effect which enables the reader to appreciate the nostalgia with which Soyinka re-creates the smells, sounds and sights of indigenous victuals which appealed to him as a child. To sustain this sensory appeal that reinforces the rhythm of the passage, and serves as the background to the various sounds we hear in it, Soyinka gradually adds one detail after another. This is quite evident, for example, in the fourth sentence where the 'oil impregnated flavours' of the akara, the 'tang of roasting coconut slices within farina cakes' and the '"high", rotted-cheese smells of *ogiri*', all of which form a vital part of the unmistakably 'oozing' aromas of the markets, contribute effectively to the sensory effect. Moreover, the poetry is enhanced by the copious use of alliteration, for example, in 'flavours . . . fully' of the first sentence; in 'fried . . . frills', 'flavours filled', cakes we called Kasada' of the fourth sentence and in 'sights . . . smells' of the last sentence.

Consider also:

> The smells are gone. In their place, mostly sounds . . . . The smells have been overcome. And their conqueror, sound, is not even the measured chimes of the tower-clock of the parade of egungun, police-bands, market cries or

bicycle-bell but a medley of electronic bands and the raucous clang of hand-bells advertising bargain sales of imported wares. (p. 149)

Soyinka creates rhythm through repetition, through the repeated use of 'the smells' at the beginning of the first and third sentences which express the same idea though with a variation in phrasing which also enhances rhythm. The rhythmic beauty of the passage is equally effected through the brevity of these sentences which echo Soyinka's love for what was. They are deliberately used to contrast the fourth long sentence which clearly conveys what has been now, that is the unpleasant sounds that have replaced the appealing smells of the past. To show his dislike for the new sounds that have overcome the old smells of the markets, Soyinka uses cacophonic words as evident, for instance, in 'a medley of electronic bands and the raucous clang of hand-bells advertising bargain sales of imported wares'. The cacophonic consonant 'k' in 'raucous clang' suggests the confusion of the hand-bells. In addition, 'raucous' and 'clang' are onomatopoeic words used to establish the disharmony that now characterizes the world of Aké's parsonage. Soyinka's displeasure can be better appreciated if the passage is read aloud when the alliterative effect is discovered: '*b*icycle *b*ell but . . . *b*ands', 'pla*c*e, mo*s*tly *s*ound*s*', '*s*ound i*s* . . . chime*s*', 'crie*s* bi*c*ycle-bell . . . band*s*' and '*s*ales of ware*s*'. The 'b' and 's' sounds noticed in these instances may suggest a combination of mellifluous sounds, but they are subdued by the harsh sounds of the 'electronic bands' and 'hand-bells'. The sound effectively evokes Soyinka's feeling of intense displeasure at the changes that have taken place in the markets where 'the blare of motor-horns and the outpouring of rock and funk and punk and other thunk-thunk from lands of instant-culture heroes' (p. 157) have replaced Dayisi's guitar and the *egungun* of old, and where the products of McDonald's and Kentucky have brought their foreign smells and tastes to dislodge the aromas and flavours that, in his childhood and youth, formed the attraction that the markets had had for him (Olney, 1983: 87). Repetition – 'thunk-thunk' and rhyme – 'rock and funk and plunk' – point the effect.

Ezekiel Mphahlele similarly uses sound to match feeling or sense in a poetic presentation. Here is a typical passage from *Down Second Avenue*:

An ominous scream pierced into the darkness of the night. I was kicking my legs about for any slight glimpse of a torchlight. I think now how harassing that torchlight was. It was like this: Saturday night and police whistles; Saturday night and screams; Saturday night and cursing from the whiteman's lips. Yet one never seemed to get used to it that the experience became commonplace and dull from beginning to end. (p. 41)

In the above description of Saturday night in a Black South African location (Marabastad), Mphahlele uses sound patterns to convey the sorrow and misery of the Blacks in South Africa, for example, the consonantal 's' sound: 'An ominou*s* scream pier*c*ed into the darkne*ss* of the night.' The cacophony of the 's' sounds suits the ugly situation that is being described, that is the physical and emotional violence suffered by the Blacks. The 's' sounds in conjunction with other consonantal sounds like 'h' and 't – 'I think now how harassing that torch-light was' – contribute effectively to the sound effect. They suggest the violence suffered by the Blacks, but they also along with repetition enhance the aesthetic appeal of the passage: 'Saturday night and police whistles; Saturday night and screams; Saturday night and cursing from the whiteman's lips.'

The quick succession of sentences with their racy rhythm graphically captures the urgency of the situation. Thus rhythm conveys Mphahlele's intense bitterness and anxiety aroused by the repetitive harassment and the harrowing conditions to which the whites subject him and his people in the violent and crippling world of South Africa. Like the Soyinka passage, this is not a mere description but a highly poetic piece.

Laye and Gatheru also re-create setting poetically. Although their approach is different from one another's and from Soyinka's and Mphahlele's, their purpose, like that of these two writers, is to achieve aesthetic satisfaction. The following rice harvest scene from *The African Child* is quite revealing:

> The tom-tom, which had been following us as we advanced into the field, kept time with our singing. We sang like a choir, often very high, with great bursts of melody, and sometimes very low, so low that we could hardly be heard. And our weariness would disappear, the heat grow less. If, on such occasions, I paused for a moment and gazed at the reapers, the long, sinuous line of reapers, I would be struck, delightfully touched, even enraptured in fact, by the tenderness, the vast, infinite tenderness in their eyes, by the immense serenity of their gaze – and that does not mean it was remote or preoccupied – as they looked about them from time to time. And yet, although they all seemed to me at such moments 'miles away' from what they were doing, their skill never faltered; the dark hands and the glittering sickles kept moving with an unbroken, almost abstracted precision. (p. 50)

In this description Laye concentrates on the details of how the people collectively relate with the landscape and with one another. The singing and beating of the tom-tom graphically illustrate the mood of un-challenged tranquility as well as the communal harmony of village life. For Laye in particular, harvesting rice becomes a sublime artistic experience. In fact, in this imaginative re-creation of the rice landscape, childhood actor and adult author are united, but it is the former's powerful inner feelings that are reflected.

The passage is most appealing even in translation because of its musicality and rhythm which have been created through the use of onomatopoeia 'tom-tom', repetition 'very low, so low', parallelism 'And yet, although they all seemed to me at such moments "miles away" from what they were doing, their skill never faltered; the dark hands and the glittering sickles kept moving with an unbroken, almost abstracted precision' and elaborative synonyms 'We sang like a choir, often very high, with great bursts of melody, and sometimes very low, so low that we could hardly be heard.' The general trend of the description, however, suggests that Laye is more interested in creating a pictorial rather than a sound effect:

> If, on such occasions, I paused for a moment and gazed at the reapers, the long, sinuous line of reapers, I would be struck, *delightfully* touched, even enraptured in fact, by the tenderness, the *vast, infinite* tenderness in their eyes, by the *immense* serenity of their gaze. (pp. 50–1)

The pictorial effect here is evident in the posture of the observer as well as that of the observed. Through his well-focused gaze the observer allows us to see the physique of the reapers: the 'infinite tenderness in their eyes', and 'immense serenity of their gaze'.

Elaboration is effectively used as in the passage (p. 26) describing his father turning gold into trinkets. While there elaboration is used rhetorically to make us believe that the father is engaged in a spiritual, other-worldly exercise, here it is used poetically to enhance the pictorial effect. The lofty adjectives italicized above reinforce the elaboration and serve as a leitmotif to underscore the 'full and deeply poetic life' (Gleason, 1965:110) of the landscape and the adults around him. The following passage achieves a similar effect:

> They were bound to one another, united by the same soul; each and every one was tasting the delight, savouring the common pleasure of accomplishing a common task. Was this delight, this pleasure, even more than the fight against weariness and against the burden of the heat, that urged them on, that filled them to over-flowing with rapturous songs? Such was obviously the case: and this is what filled their eyes with so much tenderness, that wonderful serenity that used to strike me with much delight and rather regretful astonishment; for though I was among them, with them, surrounded by these waves of tenderness, I was not one of them: I was only a school boy on a visit – and how I longed to forget that fact. (p. 51)

Here the link between the individual, society and the ethos of communalism, is conveyed by Laye's poetic evocation which takes the form of authorial comment as well as actual description of the scene. This is similarly reinforced by elaboration, but what strikes one here is the development of an idea by a simple but repetitive re-phrasing. For example: 'They were bound to one another, united by the same soul; each and every one was tasting the delight, savouring the common pleasure of accomplishing a common task.' 'United by the same soul' conveys a similar idea as 'They were bound to one another' which it is supposed to reinforce. 'Each' and 'every' in the second part of the sentence have the same meaning. Either of these determiners can be left out of the sentence or phrase and the meaning will still be retained. The same thing applies to 'tasting the delight' and 'savouring the common pleasure . . .' If the sentence was re-written without the parallels, the general meaning would remain, but the rhythmic effect which is achieved by the strategic use of repetition, elaboration and parallel constructions characteristic of several other passages will be lost and with it, its aesthetic appeal.[3]

Despite all that has been said above, what makes this scene special is Laye's feeling of separation, as a boy, from the 'full and deeply poetic life' of the rice landscape and from the adults around him.

A similar passage which describes group farming in Gatheru's *Child of Two Worlds* is rendered differently and does not evoke the type of feeling and mood noticed in Laye's:

> Sometimes after the crops had been planted, and while Mother was waiting for them to grow large enough to cut or pull or dig, she would come to the fields where I was herding to bring me food or water. But usually she was too busy for that. Kikuyu women work very hard, cultivating their crops and carrying firewood or water. Sometimes they work together in groups, helping each other. Such groups have a name *ngwatio*. Often I have heard a group of women working together and singing as they worked – making up songs about things that had happened, or boasting or joking through the words they sang, like this:
>
> LEADER   Tuinire muciare kibura (let us sing for those who are born Ethaga).
>
> CHORUS: Huuh-hoo-aaae-ii-huuh-hioo (Yes, it is so). (p. 20)

Although the simple joy of group-farming seen here is similar to that portrayed in *The African Child*, the event is not as vividly and feelingly realized. Moreover, although the feeling of comradeship and shared labour is conveyed here, that vital, though inexplicable, link between the individual and his environment found in Laye is missing. In fact, what interests Gatheru in the above description is not the affinity of the individual with the landscape but the group feeling and expression of joy that attends farm work. It is basically this he feels nostalgic about and recalls:

> Sometimes the line grew large with ten or fifteen people, and nobody wanting to admit that he was tired. These were happy days, and still today I sometimes think with sadness of this life that I shall never know again, and that, now my children will never know. (p. 21)

The elegaic tone of lost happiness discernible here is similar to the expression of regret implicit in the last Laye passage quoted above, but unlike in Laye's it is less individualistic since Gatheru uttered it on behalf of himself and others.[4]

Furthermore, unlike Laye who uses elaboration and a chain of connected phrases plus other devices to achieve aesthetic effect, Gatheru uses shorter sentences. Thus brevity does not detract from the poetic effect he achieves and sustains through the deliberate use of the 'or' in 'to cut or pull or dig'; 'food or water'; 'or boasting or joking' and 'ing' in 'herding to bring'; 'working . . . and singing'; 'cultivating . . . and carrying'; 'boasting or joking' sounds. Read aloud, it will be fully appreciated that the euphonious effect matches the group feeling and expression of joy that attends farm work which Gatheru recalls.

What has emerged from the discussion so far is that poeticization of setting in African literary autobiography is achieved through lyrical evocations and highly expressive descriptions and through the use of sound effects and other poetic devices including alliteration, consonance, personification, repetition, elaboration, parallelism.

## The use of dialogue to re-create setting

A major source of interest in *The African Child* and *Child of Two Worlds*, unlike in the other narratives, is Laye's and Gatheru's use of dialogue to create mood or atmosphere. This is illustrated in the scene in Gatheru's *Child of Two Worlds*, where his grandfather consults Kanyita, the mugo, to know his (grandfather's) fate after the theft of his protective *mwano* (medicine basket):

> When Kanyita heard the story, he laid a leather goat-skin at one corner of his yard near the thingira. My grandfather sat on a stool in front of him . . .
> At last Kanyita spoke.
> 'Son of Nguuru,' he called my grandfather respectfully and seriously.
> 'Your tragedy is great. Your *mwano* has been stolen not by an ordinary thief but by one who knows you very well, your rival and dangerous enemy.'
> 'What must I do now?' asked my grandfather.
> 'A spotless ram must be sacrificed to purify your family from the bad medicine and cleanse the footprints left in your yard by the culprits. You must then have another *mwano* conferred on you by two or more medicine-men, after which you and your entire family must go to another part of the country. You see, when your enemies got hold of your *mwano* they walked around your entire household with it – to poison you with your own magic so that all of you would die.' My grandfather was panic-stricken, particularly when he heard the second part of Kanyita's decree. All the family were upset by Kanyita's words. (pp. 197–8)

The matter-of-fact way in which the oracular decree is uttered and in which the portentous atmosphere is presented, plus the complete absence of scepticism which helps to reinforce the people's belief in the supernatural, endear the passage to the reader. Indeed, Gatheru succeeds in using dialogue here to convey the sad and grim atmosphere as well as the paradox that is his traditional society. The villagers, whether in 'Kwa Maitho', Stoton or Londioni, live an entirely integrated community life, but this can be disrupted from time to time by inimical forces, as revealed above. Malevolent spirits and their equally bad human representatives exist side by side with benevolent spirits and their equally good human representatives.

In conveying all these impressions, Gatheru uses a free, direct style, and avoids descriptive details (as he does throughout the text). He merely allows the situation he is recalling to speak for itself. By this means the reader is invited to form his own opinion and arrive at his own judgement. This is hardly a description or narrative but rather a skilful and tacit use of dialogue to convey the setting through the ' "mood" landscape'⁵ of profound silence and uncanny mysticism as well as apprehensions of the family.

Laye similarly employs dialogue in *The African Child* as in the following passage:

> This night was to be the night of Konden Diara . . .
> 'Well?' asked my father.
> He had crossed the workshop without my hearing him.
> 'Are you afraid?'
> 'A little,' I replied.
> He laid his hand on my shoulder.
> 'It's all right. Don't worry!'
> He drew me to him, and I could feel his warmth; it warmed me, too, and I began to feel less frightened, my heart did not beat fast.
> 'I, too, went through this test;' said my father.
> 'What happens to you?' I asked.
> 'Nothing you need really be afraid of, nothing you cannot overcome by your own willpower.
> Remember: you have to control your fear, you have to control yourself. Konden Diara will not take you away; he will roar; but he won't do more than roar. You won't be frightened, now, will you?'
> 'I'll try not to be.' (p. 80)

The dialogue here conveys with ease and conviction a sense of mystery or the supernatural which reinforces the idyllic quality of life in *The African Child*. Konden Diara, like the initiation ceremony Laye describes in chapter eight, is, among other things, an ordeal of fear (induced by roaring and darkness) which children like him must not only undergo, but also overcome, if they want to pass into adulthood. Indeed, Laye, like Gatheru, does not give us a piece of dialogue for its own sake but the spectacle of a situation in which verbal exchange is well manipulated to convey setting. This is even more explicit in the following passage:

> 'Each one follows his own destiny, my son. Men can do nothing to change it. This opportunity is within your reach: you must seize it ; . . .' We sat for a long time without saying anything under the veranda, looking out into the night. Then suddenly my father said in a broken voice:
> 'Promise me that you will come back?'

'I shall come back;' I said.

'These distant lands . . .' he whispered slowly.

He left the phrase unfinished: he went looking out into the darkness. I could see him by the light of the storm-lantern, looking out into the night as if at a fixed point, and frowning as if he was dissatisfied or uneasy at what he saw there.

'What are you looking at?' I asked.

'Beware of ever deceiving any one,' he said.

'Be upright in thought and deed. And God shall be with you.'

Then he made what seemed a gesture of despair, and turned his eyes away from the darkness. (p. 153)

This colloquy between Laye and his father takes place on the eve of Laye's departure for further education. The significant consideration here is not the discussion of destiny, which is an important theme in the narrative, but the general mood of sadness (especially for Laye's father) which the uneasy conversation creates. There is the subtle feeling that he sees his son's destiny entangled in the frightful associations of night and darkness. When he advises Laye to be 'upright in thought and deed' and prayerfully adds 'And God shall be with you' as he gazes into the darkness, the reader senses his worry that his son might be tempted to grope about in moral blindness in Paris. The light of the storm-lantern does not contrast but emphasizes this darkness that unnerves him.

The conversations quoted above may be fictional re-creations written several years later than they might have occurred but they seem quite convincing and honestly presented.

## Linguistic simplicity and complexity and their influence on the artistic appeal of the autobiographies

Just as these autobiographers strive to heighten meaning through richness of language achieved, for example, through poeticization of setting so also do they attempt to make their narratives appealing through simple, plain writing; writing that is straightforward from the point of view of syntactic construction; writing whose second hallmark is linguistic simplicity despite any underlying grammatical complexity one may notice in a few cases, particularly in Soyinka's. In writing simply the writers are able to achieve specificity and make their descriptions vivid. In fact they find it easier to achieve these effects through this simple writing that is neither difficult nor laborious for the reader. In *Down Second Avenue*, for example, this is how Mphahlele emphasizes the poverty and squalor and the lack of food he experienced in Maupaneng, his childhood village:

I was compelled to put on rags for a stretch of many weeks until they became a nest of lice. I'd sit out in the veld scraping off the eggs and crushing lice between the nails of my fingers. I gave up trying to wash the rags in river water. Yet I don't remember ever falling ill except for occasional stomach upsets caused by eating prickly pears excessively. The only remedy for a constipated stomach after a feast of pears was a sharpened stick pushed in through the anus and turned round and round. Castor oil and other laxatives were practically unknown for loosening the bowels. (p. 21)

Furthermore:

The only time we tasted tea and bread was when our mother came to see us at Christmas. . . . If hunting was bad we didn't have meat. About the only time we had goat's meat or beef was when livestock died. . . . I can never forget the stinking carcasses we feasted on. Often we just ate practically dry boiled corn. (pp. 18–19)

Such clarity in construction and diction does not blur or fog the writer's thoughts; neither does it tamper with a reader's understanding of what is being said or described. Such expressions as 'crushing lice between the nails of my fingers', 'stomach upset caused by eating prickly pears excessively', 'sharpened stick pushed in through the anus and turned round and round', and 'stinking carcasses we feasted on', apart from their vividness, intensify the experience by appealing to the senses of hearing, feeling and smell. Mphahlele writes like this throughout the narrative mostly when he is less personal; when he is describing events or writing about other people.

Abrahams' *Tell Freedom* similarly achieves tension through the use of brief sentences and phrases, as in the following passage:

The yard was tiny: no more than six yards wide, and yet as long. And in it, taking up half the space, was a high pile of junk: twisted bicycle wheels, old tyres, a bicycle frame, broken chains, part of an iron bed, broken with rust; pots and pans and pieces of broken crockery: rags and bones; and much other rubbish beyond recognition. (p. 57)

The brief sentences and phrases vividly and urgently suggest the squalor of the setting. It is as if the sight is too sickening to dwell on for long. Moreover, and perhaps more importantly, the use of colons and semi-colons is strategic. They are not used in the passage necessarily to differentiate a set of listed items from one another but to emphasize how the life of the people who live in this type of environment has been dislocated and immersed in decay and filth. Thus the hurried listing of unpleasant items of junk reflects the author's disgust with the nauseating list and his haste to get over these items quickly and move on to something else.[6]

This manner of writing is also seen in the section of the book (pp. 287–300) where Abrahams describes the terrible Cape Flats, although there the sentences are more varied and the structures seem more concentrated.

Of particular interest from this point of view of linguistic simplicity is Gatheru's *Child of Two Worlds* whose major hallmark, its economy, is particularly noticed in his simple vocabulary and choice of sentences which are always very brief and whose punctuations are generally easy to follow; often the sentences are without any intruding or digressive parentheses. This economy of Gatheru's style is in a way similar to what we find in *Tell Freedom*. To say this, however, does not in any way suggest that it often shares the characteristically tense staccato manner of the latter's clipped sentences. A passage from *Child of Two Worlds* that illustrates my point is the following where Gatheru shows us the part which superstition and the supernatural play in the life of his people. In the passage we specifically see how the people of. Stoton struggle in vain to check the menace of sorcerers who disturb their peace and sense of communality:

> One day a boy of one of our friends in Stoton died suddenly in the evening hours. Mwando and Kimani were called at once. They suggested that the boy's body should not be sent into the bush right away, but that it should be kept at a distance of about one mile from the village. The plan was that a group of young men armed with pangas should accompany Mwando, Kimani, and the boy's relatives to the spot where the dead boy's body was so that they could catch the sorcerer. They also hoped that they would bring the dead boy home alive! This sounds pretty fantastic, but the rumour had it that before a sorcerer cuts a piece of flesh from his victim he first of all has to bring the dead person to life again, ask him or her several questions such as: 'Who brought you here?' 'Would you like to curse your people?' and then order: 'Do not look at me.' The sorcerer would then re-poison the person, cut some flesh, and go away.
>
> They thought that they would wait until the sorcerer brought the boy back to life and when questioning started, capture him instantly. Mwano, Kimani and the rest of the young men sat down silently as if they were soldiers near the enemy line. Unfortunately, no sorcerer appeared. They sat for hours, and at about three in the morning they went home leaving the dead boy behind. At about eleven in the morning some young men went there to see the dead boy's body. On arrival there at the place they found the dead boy's body had been cut! This accelerated the fear among people tremendously. Many people decided to leave Stoton for sóme neighbouring farms. (pp. 54–5)

The passage, as it appears to me, attests to the fact that Gatheru, like many good autobiographers, has a fine memory which intimately recollects scenes from childhood. He describes things as he purportedly saw and knew them or as he was supposedly told. In trying to make the account clear and vivid, and in trying to make the reader believe him he resorts to a manner of expression that does not appear to betray him. In the above passage, his simple, unaffected, unlaborious and precise prose, which is generally devoid of syntactic complexity, helps to re-create in a kind of 'thrilling', straightforward and 'absolutely frank'[7] way the atmosphere of uncanny mysticism which pervaded the cemetery or grove to which the dead boy was taken. Throughout the narrative such intimate details of his tribal background are recounted with precision and with the minimum of words. Such precise, straightforward writing as seen, in fact, throughout *Child of Two Worlds* cannot but make us recall the following comment of the Nigerian novelist Kole Omotoso in regard to the kind of writing he wishes to practise:

> Simplicity of language . . . is one of the most important characteristics of any literature whose appeal must be to the masses of the people. (Qtd in Balogun p. 111)

Gatheru's remarkable simplicity of language also brings to mind the following comment by the English philosopher John Locke in which he identifies three ends of language:

> to make known one man's thought or idea to another; to do it with as much ease and quickness as possible, and thereby to convey the knowledge of things. (Qtd in Enekwe p. 73)

Gatheru by and large succeeds in this regard. So also do the other writers other than Soyinka.

The complications that develop in respect of Soyinka have to do with the occasional obscurity of his ideas and the complexity of his syntax, for example:

> On a misty day, the steep rise towards Itoko would join the sky. If God did not actually live there, there was little doubt that he descended first on its crest, then took his one gigantic stride over those babbling markets which dared to sell on Sundays – into St. Peter's Church, afterwards visiting the parsonage for tea with the Canon. There was the small consolation that, in spite of the temptation to arrive on horseback, he never stopped first at the Chief's, who was known to be a pagan; certainly the Chief was never seen at a church service except at the anniversaries of the Alake's coronation. Instead God strode straight into St. Peter's for morning service, paused briefly at the afternoon service, but reserved his most formal, exotic presence for the evening service which, in his honour, was always held in the English tongue. The organ took on a dark, smoky sonority at evening service, and there was no doubt that the organ was adapting its normal sounds to accompany God's own sepulchral responses, with its timbre of the egungun, to those prayers that were offered to him. (*Aké*, p. 1)

Perhaps the main idea he wants to convey has to do with the sense of mystery or mysticism that pervades Aké. Perhaps he is laughing in his customary wry manner at the Christian church and religion in the way he tries to describe the image of God descending from the sky and riding on horseback to St. Peter's Church to listen to the organ that 'Took on a dark, smoky sonority' (whatever he exactly wants to convey with this phrase). It is not easy for the reader to know precisely what Soyinka is saying in this passage. His diction and syntax are responsible for this. All the words used are familiar enough, but the way they are employed or joined together to form sentences prevents us from knowing exactly what is being conveyed or whether they are expressing and inviting approval and/or disapproval of whatever is being conveyed.

The passage begins with a short sentence which has an Adjunct ('On a misty day'), Subject ('the steep rise . . .'), Predicator ('join'), Complement ('the sky') structure. The other sentences are elaborations of this first sentence. They are difficult to comprehend chiefly because of their indiscriminately applied parentheses that are couched in interruptive clauses. These are supposed to act as modifiers, yet they impair readability and make it difficult for the reader to know what is exactly taking place. Niyi Osundare's comment on Soyinka's sentences in *The Interpreters* would also apply here: ' . . . complexly subordinated and convoluted . . . because they are characterized by highly interruptive structures that slow down the eye and hamper comprehension. . . . The reader feels tortured and is forced . . . into yawning despair' (p. 36).

The sentences of a writer like Camara Laye offer a useful contrast to Soyinka's. Laye also uses a large number of clause parentheses, but these are positively employed as modifiers or elaborations of an idea. In fact the reader does not get the impression that they are interruptions which 'hamper comprehension':

> These flatteries had an additional effect: they kept me from thinking of the sadness I felt. They had made me smile – before they began to embarrass me – but, even though my companions, too, had felt how ridiculous they were – it was natural that they should feel how ridiculous they were – they allowed nothing of this to appear on their faces; perhaps we are so accustomed to the hyperboles of our praise-singers that we no longer take very much notice of them. (*The African Child*, p. 118)

Furthermore:

> A former apprentice of my father's, who had been told I was passing through the town, had offered me hospitality for the night. This apprentice had written in the most affectionate terms; actually – but perhaps he had forgotten the difference in climate – he lodged me in a dark hut on top of a hill, where I had ample leisure – more than I wanted – to experience the chill nights and the keen air of the Fouta-Djalon. Mountains certainly did not agree with me! (*The African Child*, p. 121)

Unlike in Soyinka's work, the parenthetical elaborations, mostly indicated in pairs of dashes, are straightforward, add more information to what we already know and thus enhance our comprehension.

To test the clarity of Soyinka's thought in the above-quoted passage I gave it to my first year English Honours students for possible interpretation. All of them unabashedly confessed that they could not tell what Soyinka was really trying to say. To them, the passage was vague, and the description suffered from lack of specificity. On the other hand, their reaction to the passages from Mphahlele, Abrahams, Gatheru and Laye were quite different; they could reasonably describe and interpret the situations the writers have re-created. But this vagueness or lack of specificity noted above by me and the students in respect of this particular Soyinka passage does not detract from the overall aesthetic quality of *Aké*. If anything, it demonstrates that Soyinka, alone of these writers, varies his choice of language at least from the poetically satisfying to the syntactically or linguistically complex.

What we can say from the preceding discussion is that simple writing is good writing, and that it is one of the virtues of the African literary autobiography as demonstrated in the examples cited from Mphahlele, Abrahams, Gatheru and even Laye.

## NOTES

1. Tony E. Afejuku, 'Language as sensation: the use of poetic and evocative language in five African autobiographies', *Language and Style* 23.2 (1990): 217–26.
2. For more details, see Robert Fraser, 'Dimension of personality: elements of the autobiographical mode' in *Autobiographical and Biographical Writing in the Commonwealth*, ed. Doirean McDermot (Sabbadell, Barcelona: Editorial AUSA, 1984): 87.
3. I have argued elsewhere ('Language as Sensation . . .' p. 218) that these poetic devices are also evident in the original version in French.
4. The points and material employed and discussed here in respect of *Child of Two Worlds* are also used, although in a different context, in an earlier essay. See Tony E. Afejuku, 'Cultural assertion in the African autobiography', *Journal of Asian and African Studies* 33 (1987): 9–10.
5. This terminology is D. S. Bland's, but I do not apply it here in the exact sense in which he used it. Bland's terminology derives from how a description of a physical or natural environment in a narrative is used to illustrate the mood of a character. See, for instance, his 'Endangering the reader's neck: background description in the novel' in *Theory of the Novel*, ed. Philip Stevick (New York: The Free Press, 1976): 319.
6. The words used immediately after the preceding quotation from *Tell Freedom* up to this point are similarly employed in a forthcoming essay in *Phylon*.
7. The Kenyan novelist Ngugi wa Thiong'o and Aminu Abdullahi, a Nigerian radio journalist, who was interviewing the former for radio in London in 1964, described the book in those terms. See eds, Dennis Duerden and Cosmo Pieterse, *African Writers Talking: A Collection of Interviews* (1972; rpt. London: Heinemann, 1978): 126.

## WORKS CITED

Abrahams, Peter. *Tell Freedom*. 1954; rpt. London: Faber and Faber, 1981.

Balogun, Odun F. 'Populist fiction: Omotoso's novels'. *African Literature Today*. 13 (1983): 98–121.

Enekwe, Ossie Onuora. 'Wole Soyinka as a novelist'. *Okike*. 9 (1975): 72–86.

Gatheru, Mugo R. *Child of Two Worlds*. 1964; rpt. London: Heinemann, 1975.

Gleason, Judith Illsley. *This Africa: Novels by West Africans in English*. Evanston: North Western University Press, 1965.

Laye, Camara. *The African Child*. Trans. James Kirkup. London: Fontana, 1955.

Mphahlele, Ezekiel. *Down Second Avenue*. 1959; rpt. London: Heinemann, 1975.

Olney, James. 'Wole Soyinka as autobiographer'. *The Yale Review.* 73.1 (1983): 72–91.

Osundare, Niyi. 'Words of iron, sentences of thunder: Soyinka's prose style'. *African Literature Today.* 13, (1983): 24–37.

Pound, Ezra. 'Interludes'. In *The Modern Stylists.* Ed. Donald Hall. London: Heinemann, 1978.

Soyinka, Wole. *Aké: The Years of Childhood.* London: Rex Collings, 1981.

Traore, Ousseynou B. 'Like a mask, dancing'. *The Literary Griot.* 1.1 (1988): v–x.

## 'While she watered the morning glories':[1] Evaluating the literary achievement of Gcina Mhlophe

### Devarakshanam Betty Govinden

While the feminist debate about 'the subject', or sense of self, is illuminated in the works of several South African women writers, both black and white, it is in the writings of black women that the question of a sense of self straddles issues of race, class and gender. Black women writers such as Ellen Kuzwayo and Miriam Tlali reveal in their work the interplay of competing assumptions about the identity and role of woman and mother, intermeshed in varying strands of theoretical, feminist and nationalist discourses. In her analysis of black women writers, and with particular reference to Kuzwayo, Dorothy Driver notes that 'some space is being claimed for the voices of women beyond the careful definitions of mother in the discourse of Black Consciousness . . .' and suggests that this 'space' is taken up by Gcina Mhlophe, projecting the 'figure of "new" black woman'.[2] In this essay I shall consider the writing of Gcina Mhlophe, with a particular analysis of *Have You Seen Zandile?*,[3] in her development of an independent and critical voice.

Gcina Mhlophe [her full first name is Nokugcina] was born in KwaZulu-Natal in 1958, and developed her talents for writing at primary school and at high school. In her writings she draws from her own experience. The story *My Dear Madam*[4] published in 1981, was composed from diary entries she had made when she worked for a woman for 37 days. *Have You Seen Zandile?* has autobiographical elements, with the story of her life with an elderly aunt (depicted as a grandmother in the play) and mother. Her aunt, who was a good storyteller, had a major benevolent maternal influence on her. Gcina Mhlophe's experiences included working at film making, news reading, journalism and writing for a worker audience. She states that she has a special feeling for words and for working with words, and wishes to dispel stereotypes one may have of black performance: 'Sometimes people have this assumption that if something is black, then it must have music, it must have dancing. I love words, I think there is so much you can do in connecting with the audience without having music'.[5]

While *Have You Seen Zandile?* does have song and music, Gcina Mhlophe notes that the songs are not racy but intimate, between a girl and her grandmother – 'nothing to do with the usual energetic stuff'.[6] She also points to the significance of teenage dances in the play, where the young people are conscious of their bodies. The need to love oneself, to love one's body is important, as Mhlophe points out. With children there is less self-consciousness about the body, and more readiness at 'abandoning the body'.[7]

Gcina Mhlophe is clear that she wishes to claim a personal space or self as person/writer/performer. With the pressure to write about the masses, about larger political themes, and produce 'political theatre', she records that she has been criticized for concentrating on private concerns. Her reply is significant, for it shows that one cannot separate the personal and public: 'I argue that if I am allowed to talk about the rest of South Africa, I'm more than allowed to talk about myself. *I am one of those masses* we talk about all the time, why not talk about me specifically . . ..  My writing centres around people more than the movements . . .'.[8] She finds a public self or voice ironically by being herself.

Her independent voice is illustrated in a piece entitled *Somdaka;*[9] it is about a man Mhlophe met in Mt Frere, who was not the typical black worker in the migrant labour system. She states that she could have 'set it up in protest style', with the use of authentic migrant workers, and the help of the Mineworkers' Union. The play, *Somdaka*, is not overtly political with all the dramatic effects of spectacle, such as marching, and revolutionary songs, and shouts of 'amandlas'. But as the playwright explains, she 'wanted to get to the heart of the man'.[10]

Njabulo Ndebele has made important critical statements, that resonate immediately with Gcina Mhlophe's purposes. He has stressed the need to present the interior lives of black people and has lamented that 'writers can themselves be encapsulated by the material and intellectual culture of oppression'.[11] He called for less prescriptive approaches in black writing and the need for critical distance. He makes the important point that writers are trapped in the very society they are criticizing, with the result that they unwittingly normalize apartheid. His dictum, the 'rediscovery of the ordinary', has become a critical touchstone in South African literary criticism, where he calls for the depiction of black lives in their particularity rather than the 'human anonymity' that is, in fact, a dimension of the oppressor's strategy.[12] Ndebele's call for a radical displacement of the white oppressor as an active, dominant player in the imagination of the oppressed[13] is well illustrated in Gcina Mhlophe's approach to her art and her sense of self.

What Gcina Mhlophe does is side-step the power games involved in cultural resistance to apartheid; she forges a 'liberated zone' through her writing, outside the regimes of truth of apartheid. She resists packaging one-dimensional, reductionist caricatures of political history. While she goes back to the wellsprings of culture, lost through urbanization, this is not a romanticized life of a remote past, but a life that is very contemporary. The tendency to compartmentalize people into rural and urban is resisted, as Gcina Mhlophe shows the way in which the lives of people from these two sectors are inextricably linked. In bridging the gap between rural and urban naturally, she dispels stereotypes of rural women. Lauretta Ngcobo notes that when rural women are mentioned there is a response such as: 'You mean the ones who carry wood on their heads?'.[14] Of Gcina Mhlophe she observes, 'I think it is her rural background that makes her as rich as she is . . .'[15] Nor is rural life idealized. In *Nokulunga's Wedding*[16] Mhlophe uses irony to show the entrapment of a black woman in traditional black society: 'There is nothing to be done'. Driver argues that in this short story Gcina Mhlophe 'exposes the voices of patriarchy that preside over the oral tradition, and thus exposes the voice of communal orality as a voice which curbs and controls female desire'.[17] One reads the silences of the text, its inevitability, critically.

Gcina Mhlophe draws from black women's experiences. Elaine Showalter[18] distinguishes between feminine (imitative of men's writing), feminist (protest against oppression) and female writing (the use of female experience as the source of their art). Gcina Mhlophe uses female experience as the context to protest against oppression, devising various strategies that are in keeping with the circumstances of women. Cecily Lockett refers to Mhlophe as 'probably the most overtly feminist of the black poets now writing'.[19] In the poem 'Say No' Mhlophe is strident that women should resist all forms of oppression:

Say No, Black Woman
Say No
When they give you a back seat
in the liberation wagon
Say No
Yes Black Woman
a Big NO[20]

A different resolution is sought in her piece 'The Toilet',[21] which relates the problems a black woman encounters in finding a physical and metaphorical space in which to write. She draws from autobiographical details as she herself was confined to a back room in the house where her sister was a domestic employee. The story highlights the importance of making choices, and that black women cannot be passive, but must become agents of their own destiny. In 'The Toilet' Gcina Mhlophe does not project a 'victim-image' of black women but shows their determination to overcome obstacles. The physical problem of finding space to write is general for black women: 'Living, in this our country, has made massive cultural and historical demands on us, so that the mere act of writing, of finding time, let alone space to do so, is in itself an act of monumental significance'.[22]

The underlying significance of finding a writing-space is noted by Driver, who states that 'Mhlophe's narrative ... is about finding a position from which to write, which is to say about constructing an identity from which to speak, a place from which she may both view herself (as writer) and her sister (she who forbids writing) and from which she may dream of a world which offers, through acting, the assumption of many more roles than a wife who makes baby clothes and does not read too much'.[23] In the short story she feels the pull of the womb of security provided by the toilet: 'the walls were wonderfully close to me – it felt like it was made to fit me alone'.[24] Yet if she is to grow into her own person, become a writer, she must move beyond the safe confines of such enclosure, and seek the open spaces of the wider world. This means not accepting the 'law of the father which demands her absence and silence' but engaging in nurturing oneself, to use the maternal metaphor, in one's emergence as a writer.[25]

Mhlophe's claiming of her freedom as a person and as a writer has echoes in Zoe Wicomb's depiction of Frieda in *You Can't Get Lost in Cape Town*[26], where Frieda moves from the foetal position when she hides under the kitchen table, in the short story, 'Bowl like Hole', to developing into an independent writer in the later stories.[27]

The disposition to find a unique and individual response to South African township life is shown in the short piece, 'It's Quiet Now'.[28] The narrator is depicted as a self, alone, at the window, in the middle of the night, reflecting on an earlier scene of violence. While maintaining a certain distance, she is not detached, but reflective, finding a space between a sense of self and the affairs of the community. She does not set up any binary or hierarchical divisions, and resists the fashionable preoccupation to extol 'the struggle' and the macro freedom story of black South Africans.

This shifting link between the personal and political, and Gcina Mhlophe's claiming of an individual as well as a communal voice is well illustrated in *Have You Seen Zandile?* While the play is attributed to Mhlophe, as the principal author, the script actually developed experimentally, with Mhlophe collaborating with two other women playwrights, Maralin Van Renen and Thembi Mtshali. The play begins with Zandile alone on stage, singing about MOTHERS who will be coming home bringing their children sweets, rice and meat (p. 1). We note the difference between fantasy and reality, when the imaginary sweet becomes the real stone, in her mouth. Her dreamworld is conjured up with Bongi, the imaginary companion, and concerns the important elements in her world of experience – dresses, school, and beating ... Zandile is eight years old at this point, and the inevitable question of what she will become when she grows up (p. 4) crops up.

Zandile dreams for Bongi: she will become 'a white lady with long hair like that, and you will have nice clothes and nice shoes with high heels. . . . And Bongi, we can speak English . . . you can also have a car!' (pp. 4–5). The content of her life is controlled by a distant white world, and is underlined once again when Zandile asks: 'Gogo, I love this doll but why do they always make them pink?' (p. 8). Fanon's classic observations of colonial and colonized continue to have grim validity here.

The important element of the play is that it revolves around Zandile's relationship with the women in her life. The identity of women is not connected with male figures, as in Buchi Emecheta's *The Joys of Motherhood* or Flora Nwapa's *Efuru*. While this is a world where men are absent,[29] the patriarchal world still remains intact. Her mother reminds her that she cannot perform traditional ceremonies without the male figures, and the ideal is still marrying a man, and raising children. Even Gogo sees this as the ultimate goal for Zandile: 'I can even see my little Zandile, wearing a white dress, walking slowly out of church with her husband and smiling with those dimples that I like' (p. 26). Male values also dominate education, as they study the 'white man's' history. We note the aversion to the study of this history (and biology) at school.

The absence of men, however, has the ironic value of empowering women. Women are able to provide love and an atmosphere for personal growth for other women; women provide the security to develop a positive self-image, especially when one's sense of self is undermined. To adapt the concept of *ubuntu*, one may assert that 'a woman is a woman because of another woman'. This bonding especially takes place in the context of story-telling between Zandile and Gogo, the grandmother. Kuzwayo points to the centrality of women in African folklore: 'and in all this it was the women, the mothers and the grandmothers who did the communicating, the teaching'.[30] Trinh Minh'ha also points out that 'Every woman partakes in the chain of guardianship and transmission'.[31] Gcina Mhlophe shows how each thrives on this relationship.

Other writers, such as Maya Angelou and Ama Ata Aidoo, have also depicted in their writings the pivotal role of 'the grandmother', as survivor of the extended family.[32] In Mhlophe's story the grandmother gives the child the great gift of stories and the magic to tell them, and the child gives the grandmother a purpose (p. 11). We realize later that when the grandmother dies this is due to her bereftness at Zandile's absence. The life shared between Gogo and Zandile is one of sufficiency, if not of plenty. There is no sense of abject poverty, both materially and emotionally, and the continuity in and with an oral literary community is depicted naturally. Their lives are like the ' "eet-sum-more" biscuits, the tin never goes empty . . .' (p. 3) It is ironic that the picture of the HAPPY FAMILY is a consumer image on the Mazawatee Tea tin, and the words on the 'Zulu Mottoes' – 'you are the love of my heart' (p. 15) are, in fact, true. Eva Hunter and Dorothy Driver caution us, however, from claiming a special link between women and orality, illustrating their point of view with reference to Mhlophe's *Nokulunga's Wedding*, where the predominant voice is a patriarchal one curbing the expression and will of 'female desire'.[33]

One of the stories that Gogo tells is of a woman who faces difficulties in her life, and has to work on Sundays. We have an evocative picture of a madonna figure, with a child and dog of many colours. This story links women to the origins of the cosmos unobtrusively, as the woman in the story was translated to the moon. This seems to be consonant with the 'yang' principle, of origins of life and culture, rather than the western 'man in the moon' concept. During the story-telling that transports Zandile into another, wider world, Zandile goes off to sleep in the warmth of her grandmother's words, and is undergirded by the concluding prayer, 'uJehova unguMalusi wami' which is an interesting collocation between the 'missionary faith' that arrived in the last century and the reclaiming of an earlier, older spirituality.

Zandile's imaginary experience includes lessons to her grandmother's flower-bed as a class of children, with herself as teacher. In her imagination, she will have the children's eyes gouged out (p. 19) if they do not obey her, the teacher. In her new dress with patterns of goats, giraffes and elephants, she again shows the extent that they are ruled by values from a white world – they have to change their names to white names, as they await the arrival of the white supervisor. It is ironic that the children are like sunflowers – wanting to grow – but, Zandile, styling herself along the behaviour of her own teachers, is breaking the flowers – ten years before the Soweto Revolt. Gogo reminds Zandile of the sanctity of all life – including plants (p. 23). It is ironic that it is for this educational system that Gogo is prepared to sacrifice, to give Zandile an opportunity to study. As she says: 'even if I have to die doing it, I'm keeping Zandile at school' (p. 9). The Soweto youth were prepared to die rather than continue in apartheid schools.

Zandile is forcibly removed from her world with her grandmother when the feared white car does arrive and she is snatched away to live in the Transkei with her mother, Lulama. Zandile writes letters to Gogo in the sand, hoping the birds will carry her message to her. She writes to Gogo, recalling that she used to put Zambuk on her blisters (p. 34), 'but they don't have Zambuk here . . .' (p. 34). There is a significant relational difference between Zandile and Lulama, the mother, signifying two different worlds. As Lulama points out, 'This is not Durban, this is the Transkei' (p. 38). The mother, hardened by the circumstances of her life, wants to develop a tenacious personality in Zandile. The mother also tells her 'stories', but they are of the stark reality of her own struggle to survive. 'When I was your age I cut the grass for every roof in this house' (p. 39), she points out grimly. She loves to have her daughter with her, but has been the victim of tradition and circumstances, in marrying early, and with the responsibilities of caring for four children at the age of twenty two.

It is the stories of the imagination that have helped them survive the ravages of apartheid, stories set in a rural situation rather than the urban. A victim of bureaucracy and discrimination against women, Lulama had to give up her career as a singer, and is robbed of the creative energies that sustain the imagination; Gogo had escaped the debilitating effects of this truncated living. One is aware of a romantically promising picture of the life that Lulama had, being dashed to the ground, and this constrains her to teach Zandile to work to survive, 'That is why I have learnt not to live on hopes, that is why I am teaching you to work . . .' (p. 41). Lulama's life is emotionally denuded, without dream and story. In her poem, 'The Dancer', Gcina Mhlophe writes to her 'Mama', and there are overtones with her depiction of Lulama, the mother, in *Have You Seen Zandile?*, as in her own life:

Mama
they tell me you were a dancer
they tell me you had long
beautiful legs to carry your graceful body
they tell me you were a dancer

Mama
they tell me you sang beautiful solos
they tell me you closed your eyes
always when the feeling of the song
was right, and lifted your face up to the sky
they tell me you were an enchanting dancer

Mama
they tell me you were always so gentle
they talk of a willow tree
swaying lovingly over clear running water
in early Spring when they talk of you
they tell me you were a slow dancer

Mama
they tell me you were a wedding dancer
they tell me you smiled and closed your eyes
your arms curving outward just a little
and your feet shuffling in the sand;
tshi tshi tshitshitsha tshitshi tshitshitshitsha
o hee! how I wish I was there to see you
they tell me you were a pleasure to watch

Mama
they tell me I am a dancer too
but I don't know . . .
I don't know for sure what a wedding dancer is
there are no more weddings
but many, many funerals

where we sing and dance
running fast with the coffin
of a would-be bride or would-be groom
strange smiles have replaced our tears
our eyes are full of vengeance, Mama

Dear, dear Mama
they tell me I am a funeral dancer. (1985–1988)[34]

Gcina Mhlophe paints the image of a 'prima donna', wafting on the promise of a bright future, but unable to realize her dreams. Alice Walker, in *In Search of our Mothers' Gardens*, also draws attention to the way women's hopes to become creative artists and to write about beauty are dissipated. Through the life of one individual she also shows the tragedy of the whole community, with hopes of life turned to death, in the decades that followed. In contrast to the life of the grandmother, we see the effects of urbanization on Lulama. The myth of 'Mother Africa', of which her own mother is an individual example, is explored as women are caught in the wider forces of oppression. In her poem, 'We are at War', Mhlophe writes:

Forces of exploitation
degrade mother Africa
as well as us, her daughters
Her motherly smile is ridiculed
She has seen her children sold
Her chains of slavery are centuries old
There is not time to cry now . . .[35]

Miriam Tlali, among other black women writers, has also drawn attention to the tendency to confuse 'Mother Africa' with the role of African mothers, when she states, 'It is a problem when men want to call you Mother Africa and put you on a pedestal, because they want you to stay there forever without asking your opinion – and unhappy you if you want to come down as an equal human being'.[36]

The other main relationship in the play is that between Zandile and her friend Lindiwe. They share 'stories' of their adolescent experiences, and these are in contrast with those between Zandile and her grandmother and mother. The stories are of boys and of menstruation, of the new myths of growing up – that babies came from the aeroplane – and obsessions with being fat. Zandile regrets that she cannot ask her mother for answers to her burning questions. They look forward to reading BONA and DRUM – magazines from the alternative culture – which will provide them with further 'stories' – the 'real' knowledge they desire – not the history and other subjects that are dispensed at school. Zandile notes: 'I hate history. The great trek, great trek every year it's the same, the great trek' (p. 49). Trinh Minh'ha notes that 'when history is separated itself from story, it started indulging in accumulation and facts'.[37]

The myth of an alluring life in distant Johannesburg is especially strong for Lindiwe, who dreams of meeting 'sophisticated men' there. The irony is that this is 1976, and the world of Soweto is also part of that reality. The pulp culture of Barbara Cartland is pervasive, and of American pop music, epitomized by the song 'Sugar-sugar, honey-honey, you are my candy girl', which also shows the way women are possessed by men. Zandile, however, does not see fulfilment in her life necessarily culminating in love and marriage, and this is confirmed by the promise of a different kind, as suggested in the concluding scene.

The poignant ending shows Zandile holding up a photograph, set in a Bible, and a suitcase full of presents. She holds up the dresses that her grandmother had been saving up for her, showing a longing to encapsulate her world in the beauty of childhood, of not losing one's innocence with the passage into adulthood. They also signify the timeless gift of storytelling which is the grandmother's real gift to Zandile (and to Mhlophe), and the celebration of this through the play, *Have You Seen Zandile?* Mhlophe has also subverted the 'gift' that was confined to storytelling in the (female) domestic domain by transporting it, with much acclaim, to the (male) public space of performance. It is important to note, then, that while Mhlophe weaves autobiographical elements in her writing, especially of her growing up experiences in the play, she, like Zoe Wicomb in *You Can't Get Lost in Cape Town* is not presenting an 'autobiography of nostalgia', that is directed towards some idealized past. In presenting both positive and negative experiences Mhlophe is producing 'survivor-knowledge', and creating the future.[38]

By depicting dramatically different worlds in Zandile's relationships with three central women in her life, Mhlophe is problematizing the concept of 'sisterhood' and 'motherhood' among black women, given the differences among individuals, within families, communities, and between age groups. M. J. Daymond's point that ' "motherhood" in South African writing and criticism functions as a profoundly disruptive and simultaneously reintegrative metaphor',[39] is evident in Mhlophe, but in a different, and unique configuration of relationships. Mhlophe is depicting a black woman who is developing an independence from maternal influences, as well as acknowledging a maternal figure (epitomized in the character of Gogo) as an important formative influence. In her depiction of Lulama, she is critical, too, of the 'controlling image' that all black women are 'natural' mothers.[40]

Given the closeness to details of Mhlophe's own life, and her point that the play is her way of 'exploring memory and disruption in a woman's life',[41] we see the intersection of the personal and artistic, in the effort to recuperate and assert selfhood, agency and subjectivity, rather than 'blame herself on history'.

When we compare Mhlophe with say Kuzwayo and Tlali, we notice that black women writers depict a 'variety of subjectivities'; the tendency to homogenize African women is resisted.[42] In constructing an independent, autonomous space Mhlophe has worked with the experience of 'difference' without fetishizing and celebrating it for itself.[43]

The discourse of identity and difference within feminism, based on constructed binaries and linearity between men and women, and between white and black women is modulated, even disrupted, as we consider its fluid, dynamic nature, and as we consider difference within 'difference'. In embodying a multiplicity of influences, all in interaction with one another, and projecting a complex self, as depicted in the character of Zandile, Mhlophe illustrates well the 'hyphenated identities and hybrid realities' that Trinh Minh'ha speaks of.[44]

At the same time, Mhlophe does not discount the place of solidarity among all women. In her poem 'We are at War', already referred to, she sees that 'women of my country/mother Africa's loved daughters/black and white' face a common enemy.[45] Mhlophe is stridently feminist in what she believes women can achieve from within a common solidarity shared by all women, both black and white. Yet she is claiming such a feminist position within the sphere of indigenous African, rather than western experience, and is far from producing a 'colourless' feminism.

Mhlophe's purposes are wide-ranging and critical, as she explores questions of politics, gender and race in the light of experience, and expressed through the 'participatory literature of liberation' based on the African communal experience. Her identities as writer, black woman, Third World woman, global woman are intricately interwoven in a particular temporal and spatial context. She has developed her own storytelling project (called *Zanendaba* – '*Bring me a Story*') in the context of local culture, and has also extended this art to draw from the rich heritage of folklore among the traditional literatures of the world. Mhlophe expresses a particular wish to 'reclaim Africa'. This is one of the challenges of reading and writing in the new South Africa. As Tony Voss notes 'The civil imaginary, the cultural space, the *kgotla*: much of our humanity, much of what we are able to contribute to the world will depend on our rootedness in Africa'.[46]

Gcina Mhlophe points out that when she travels she uses a translator, since her play, *Have You Seen Zandile?* is in three languages – English, Xhosa and Zulu. She wrote it naturally switching from one language to another, and the overall effect is that of a 'bridge' since it is more inclusive than if it were only in one language. In the mixing of languages she is drawing from her own language experiences, having learnt Zulu in KwaZulu-Natal from her father's family, and Xhosa in the Transkei, when she moved to be with her mother. She is able to incorporate the multi-dimensional character of the languages, and thus shows up the artificial boundaries that were set up to justify the creation of Bantustans in pursuance of 'grand apartheid'. Mhlophe's point that 'Language is who you are, it is important to say "this is my language" ' – shows the multi-faceted sense of selfhood that she is forging. She embodies the merging of different local languages and cultures, with a strong individuality in the context of her life's experiences, bridging traditional black culture and western forms, in all their heterogeneity.

In an interesting way Mhlophe is locating her work in the local and particular, and in this way reaching to the universal, across cultures and traditions. The trans-global culture that she is creating is not that of the commodity-ridden culture of Coca-Cola and Zambuk, but that of the fabric of community life, and of cultural memory, straddling rural and urban experience. Writing in another time and place, but describing Gcina Mhlophe's experiences well, Silko records: 'I grew up with storytelling. My earliest memories are of my grandmother telling me stories while she watered the morning-glories in her yard'.[47] In this way Gcina Mhlophe is contributing significantly to developing a critical feminism, an alternative new internationalism and a vibrant heterogeneous post-colonial literary culture.

## NOTES

1. Leslie Marmon Silko, quoted in Trinh T. Minh'ha, *Woman, Native, Other – Writing Postcoloniality and Feminism* (Bloomington: Indiana, 1989): 135.
2. Dorothy Driver, in M. J. Daymond, Introduction to *Feminists Reading South Africa, 1990–1994*, p. 14 (forthcoming).
3. Mhlophe, Gcina, T. Mtshali and M. van Renen, *Have You Seen Zandile?* (Johannesburg: Skotaville, 1988).
4. Gcina Mhlophe, *My Dear Madam*, in Mothobi Mutloase, *Reconstruction* (Johannesburg: Ravan Press, 1981): 180–98.
5. Gcina Mhlophe, in Interview with Dennis Walder, 'The Number of Girls is Growing', in *Contemporary Theatre Review* [Special Issue on South African Drama], November, 1995 p. 3.
6. Walder: 5.
7. Walder: 5.
8. Walder: 5.
9. *Somdaka* was written and directed by Mhlophe, at the Market Theatre, in Johannesburg, in 1989.
10. Walder: 6.
11. Njabulo Ndebele, *Rediscovery of the Ordinary – Essays on South African Literature and Culture* (Johannesburg: Congress of South African Writers [COSAW], 1991): 63.
12. Ndebele: 23.
13. Ndebele.
14. M. J. Daymond, 'Some Thoughts on South Africa, 1992: Interview with Lauretta Ngcobo', in *Current Writing* 4.1 (1992): 85–97.
15. *Current Writing*.
16. Gcina Mhlophe, *Nokulunga's Wedding*, in Susan Brown et al (eds), *LIP: from Southern African Women* (Johannesburg: Skotaville, 1987): 82–6.

17. Dorothy Driver, 'M'a-Ngoana, O Tsoare Thipa ka Bohaleng – The Child's Mother Grabs the Sharp End of the Knife: Women as Mothers, Women as Writers', in *Rendering Things Visible – Essays on South African Literary Culture*, ed. Martin Trump (Johannesburg: Ravan Press, 1990): 250.
18. Elaine Showalter, 'Towards a Feminist Poetics', in *The New Feminist Criticism*, ed. Elaine Showalter (London: Virago, 1993): 125–143.
19. *Breaking the Silence – A Century of South African Women's Poetry*, ed. Cecily Locket (Johannesburg: Ad Donker, 1990): 36.
20. Susan Brown, Isabel Hofmeyr, Susan Rosenberg (eds), *LIP from Southern African Women* (Johannesburg: Ravan Press, 1983): 164–5.
21. Gcina Mhlophe, 'The Toilet', in *Sometimes When it Rains: Writings by South African Women*, ed. Ann Oosthuizen (London: Pandora, 1987): 1–7.
22. Publisher's note in *Women in South Africa: From the Heart – An Anthology* (Johannesburg: Seriti sa Sechaba Publishers, 1988): 6.
23. Driver: 251.
24. *Sometimes When it Rains: Writings by South African Women*, ed. Ann Oosthuizen (London: Pandora, 1987).
25. See Joan Meterlerkamp, Ruth Miller: 'Father's Law or Mother's Lore?', *Current Writing* 4 (1992): 57–71.
26. Zoe Wicomb, *You Can't Get Lost in Cape Town* (London: Virago, 1987).
27. Rob Gaylard, 'Exile and Homecoming: An Approach to Zoe Wicomb's *You Can't Get Lost in Cape Town*, paper presented at the Association of University English Teachers of South Africa [AUETSA] Conference, Transkei, 1994.
28. Gcina Mhlope, 'It's Quiet Now', in Oosthuizen: 8–9.
29. Demographic figures on 'male absenteeism' in South Africa have pointed to its particular incidence in KwaZulu-Natal and the former Transkei.
30. An Introduction to *Women in South Africa: From the Heart – An Anthology* (Johannesburg: Seriti sa Sechaba Publishers, 1988): 6.
31. Minh-ha: 121.
32. See Mildred Hill-Lubin, 'The Grandmother in African and African-American Literature', in *Ngambika – Studies in Women in African Literature*, eds Carol Boyce Davies & Anne Adams (Trenton, New Jersey: Africa World Press, 1986): 241–56.
33. Eva Hunter, 'A Mother is Nothing but a Backbone – Tradition and Change', in Miriam Tlali's *Footprints in the Quag*, *Current Writing* 5.1: 60–75.
34. ed. Lockett: 352–3.
35. Brown: 159–60.
36. Quoted in Mineke Schipper, 'Mother Africa on a Pedestal: the Male Heritage in African Literature and Criticism', in *African Literature Today*, 7 (1987): 35–54.
37. Minh-ha: 119.
38. Janet Varner Gunn, ' "Border-Crossing" and the Cross-Cultural Study of Autobiography', paper presented at the Association of University English Teachers of Southern Africa [AUETSA] Conference, 1994.
39. M. J. Daymond, *Feminists Reading South Africa, 1990–1994: Writing, Theory and Criticism*, p. 9 (forthcoming).
40. Patricia Hill Collins, *Black Feminist Thought: Knowledge, Consciousness, and the Politics of Empowerment* (Boston: Unwin Hyman, 1990): 70.
41. Walder: 8.
42. Hunter: 72.
43. Edward Said draws attention to this trend among those who have been 'othered': 'Representing the Colonised: Anthropology's Interlocutors, *Critical Inquiry* 15 (Winter 1989): 213.
44. *When the Moon Waxes Red: Representation, Gender and Cultural Politics* (London: Routledge, 1991): 73.

45. Brown: 159–60.
46. Tony Voss, 'Reading and Writing in the New South Africa', *Current Writing* 4.1 (1992): 8.
47. Leslie Marmon Silko in Minh'ha: 135.

# Childhood à la Camara Laye
# & Childhood à la Mongo Beti

## E. P. Abanime

The Guinean Camara Laye and the Cameroonian Mongo Beti are undoubtedly among the best-known and most often discussed writers from· French-speaking Africa. Laye's first published work, the autobiographical novel, *L'Enfant noir*, translated into English as *The African Child*, deals with the theme of childhood in a wide sense of the word.[1] The story starts with the narrator playing in his father's compound at the age of 'five, maybe six years' (*African Child*, p. 11), and ends with him in an aeroplane on his way to France for further studies, when he must have been nineteen years old. The author's third novel *Dramouss* (*A Dream of Africa*) which appeared thirteen years later forms a sequel to *L'Enfant noir* in that it shows what the Camara of the first novel, now renamed Fatoman, does during the six years he spends in France, and on his subsequent return to his native land, but is obviously concerned with adulthood rather than with childhood, since the narrator is now in his twenties.

Denis, the narrator in *Le Pauvre Christ de Bomba* (*The Poor Christ of Bomba*), Mongo Beti's second novel and the first to appear under his now renowned pen-name,[2] would certainly be considered to be a child even though the novelist indicates that he is already almost fifteen by the time the story begins (*Poor Christ*, p. 9), and attributes to him the rather unchildly achievement of leaving 'a big gray stain' (p. 106) of semen on a bedsheet when he is inveigled into performing the sexual act with a young woman named Catherine. But the book is, as the title suggests, much more about the elderly or middle-aged Reverend Father Drumont than about the juvenile Denis. The young people in most of Mongo Beti's other novels are really adults and not children, even when, as in the case of Kris in *Le Roi miraculé* (*King Lazarus*) and of Jean-Marie Medza in *Mission terminée* (*Mission to Kala*), they are still students in secondary schools. It is in the last two of the nine novels that he has published so far, namely *Les Deux Mères de Guillaume Ismaël Dzewatama* and *La Revanche de Guillaume Ismaël Dzewatama*, which appeared in book form in 1982 and 1984 respectively, that the

Cameroonian writer manifests obvious interest in the theme of childhood.[3] The two novels recount to a considerable extent the life of Guillaume Ismaël Dzewatama from the time of his birth in 1963, or more exactly from the time of the marriage of his parents in 1962, through the time he is taken to France in the summer of what would seem to be the year 1979 to the time he is sent back to Africa at the age of nearly seventeen.

There is obviously some resemblance between Camara Laye's *L'Enfant noir* and its sequel *Dramouss* on the one hand and Mongo Beti's two novels of 1982 and 1984 on the other hand. In each of the two pairs of novels we see a black African develop from childhood to the teens, go to France – practically as an adult in the case of Laye – and then return to his native land. However, the drawing of a parallel between the creative writings of the Guinean and the Cameroonian would not go beyond that point if one were to go by the strong attack which Mongo Beti made on *L'Enfant noir* when it appeared in 1953. Reviewing the novel in an article entitled 'L'Enfant noir', which appeared in *Présence Africaine* in 1954 (no 16 of a special issue series) and which he signed with his real initials of A. B. (standing for Alexandre Biyidi), the then twenty-two-year-old Cameroonian student in France denounced the idyllic picture which the Guinean author had painted of an African society then under the yoke of French colonialism:

> Laye obstinately closes his eyes to the most crucial realities, precisely the ones that have always been hidden from the public here. Did this Guinean, a person of my race, who was, according to him, a very sharp boy, then never see anything other than a peaceful, beautiful and maternal Africa? Is it possible that not on a single occasion was Laye a witness to a single little exaction by the colonial administration? (p. 420)

Going a step further, A. B. implicitly questioned Laye's motive in publishing the novel:

> As a matter of fact, what is at issue here is much less the book as the mentality of which it is the nauseating product . . . Laye assuredly takes pleasure in the anodyne, and above all in the most facile – therefore most lucrative – picturesque, turns a hackneyed procedure into an art process. In spite of appearances it is a stereotyped – therefore false – picture of Africa and Africans that he is labouring to show: idyllic world, optimism of big infants, stupidly interminable feasts, carnival initiations, circumcisions, excisions, superstitions, Uncle Mamadous whose inconscience is only equalled by their unreality. (p. 420)

Qualifying the 'facile' picturesque in *L'Enfant noir* as 'lucrative' is in fact a way of saying that Camara Laye wrote his novel with the aim of securing a large French readership, and hence handsome royalties, by presenting what he knew that whites in general, and French people in particular, would like to read about black Africa; French-colonized black Africa itself not being fertile ground for winning a large readership (and hence fat royalties) because of its large-scale illiteracy and poverty.

It has to be admitted that Mongo Beti's way of portraying Guillaume Ismaël Dzewatama's childhood is in certain ways quite different from Camara Laye's way of portraying his fictional childhood. On the face of it, the Cameroonian author demonstrates realism in *Les Deux Mères* and *La Revanche*, contrary to the idealism which he had so harshly criticized with regard to *L'Enfant noir* in his *Présence Africaine* article of some thirty years before. That he wanted his own portrayal of African childhood to be considered to be unidealized is evident in the initial title which he gave to the first of the two Dzewatama novels when he serialized it in his journal *Peuples Noirs – Peuples Africains* in 1981 and 1982 before it appeared as a book with the imprint of Buchet/ Chastel: 'L'Enfance précaire et cahoteuse de Guillaume Dzewatama', which can be translated into English as 'The Precarious and Bumpy Childhood of Guillaume Dzewatama'.[4]

Unlike Camara Laye whose African child grows up between a loving and contented father and mother, Mongo Beti makes his Guillaume Ismaël start off as a virtually one-parent child of a victimized mother. While the child is still developing in its mother's womb, its father, Jean-François Dzewatama, who is away in France for university studies, falls out with the dictatorial regime of his African country against which he has taken a stand as a student leader. Designated a political enemy by the regime, Jean-François not only has his scholarship withdrawn but can also no longer go back home. To make matters worse, the regime at home begins to persecute members of the exiled dissident's family by way of vicarious reprisal: his aged father, his elder brother, his wife Agathe who is now six months into her pregnancy with Guillaume Ismaël. The periodic arrests and detention of innocent people by the Special Combined Brigade, the home regime's security force, continue after the birth of Guillaume Ismaël:

> When Guillaume was born cruel fun was made at the Special Combined Brigade of the sorry situation of the child and especially of the mother who was often arrested at the same time as Dzewatama father and son. From time to time the detainees were ill-treated without precise reason. One day Agathe herself was struck even though she was breast-feeding Guillaume. As if aware of the drama on its mother, the baby immediately stopped sucking the breast and gave terrible screams. (*Deux mères*, pp. 18–19)

With little prospect of being able to return to his African country, Jean-François Dzewatama marries a young Frenchwoman named Marie-Pierre Letellier, a fellow student of his at the University of Lyon – without revealing to the white woman that he is already married to a woman of his black African tribe, and a father. Guillaume Ismaël has evidently already reached adolescence when Jean-François finally returns home following an apparent reconciliation with his country's iniquitous regime, and when the father is joined several months later by his white wife and their mulatto baby boy the stage is set for what one might expect to be a particularly unhappy episode of an African child's life. Before examining how this crisis situation is resolved by Mongo Beti, let me illustrate further how, on the face of it, Camara Laye's idealism contrasts with the Cameroonian writer's realism. Whereas in real life many a child cannot escape being unpleasantly affected, at least occasionally, by overt or insidious jealousies and rivalries among women sharing one husband, the fictional Laye of *L'Enfant noir* recollects nothing but harmony among the women and children in his polygamous father's household. During the dance occasioned by preparations for the circumcision of members of his age grade, it is the second wife of his father who joins in the dance, proudly holding aloft an exercise book and a fountain pen to symbolize the intellectual competence of her stepson (*The African Child*, p. 97).

Remarkable in the matter of Laye's idealism versus Beti's realism is the experience which each of the two writers creates for his African child when the child goes to live temporarily in the village of his maternal grandparents. Camara Laye's child is, if anything, happier on the occasions he goes to Tindican to spend ten days or so with his maternal grandmother and his maternal uncles than when he is staying with his parents in his own town of Kouroussa. In the English translation of the 1953 novel, the two chapters devoted to the fictional Camara Laye's stays in his maternal grandmother's village characteristically end with a nostaligic 'Ah! How happy we were in those days!' (p. 54). Under essentially similar circumstances Mongo Beti thinks up an unhappy experience for his African child. Whereas the stays at Tindican are fattening sessions for the fictional Guinean child, the Cameroonian novelist makes Guillaume Ismaël undergo an ordeal of starvation when, at the age of about ten, he is sent to live with his maternal grandparents because their village is nearer than his own to the mission school he is attending. The hunger becomes so unbearable that Guillaume Ismaël slips off in the dead of night and walks all the way back to his own village some eight kilometres away, where he recounts his ordeal to his mother: 'Nobody was paying attention to me, except hunger, but that was only to torture me more than you can imagine, mama. I could not bear it any more. I wish to remain with you. I have suffered too much hunger' (*Deux mères*, p. 27). The child's starvation was due not only to negligence on the part of his maternal uncles and the wife of his elder maternal uncle but also to the fact that the grandparents themselves were 'retiring into the egocentric indolence so frequent among old people' (p. 28). One would no doubt have to do a good deal of searching in order to find another episode in African literature where a child is abandoned to starvation by its own grandparents – and in particular by its own grandmother – even with the excuse of senile apathy.

Even the reconciliation of the runaway Guillaume Ismaël with his maternal grandparents is far from idyllic. The grandparents do vow that they will henceforth take utmost care of the child when the latter is brought back to them. 'But,' observes the narrator, 'the spell had been broken. He was indeed coddled and pampered, but he was considered to be a little monster' (p. 28). The coddling and pampering were evidently due more to fear of being denounced to all and sundry for the neglect of a ten-year-old child than to the natural affection which one should expect from grandparents, and in particular from a grandmother.

At the end of *Les Deux Mères* Mongo Beti briefly changes from the fictional to the factual mode to reaffirm his fidelity to realism in literature. Perhaps still impelled by annoyance at the acclaim which Western critics who can make or break African literary reputations had given to Camara Laye's *L'Enfant noir*, the Cameroonian author points out in a thirty-four-line epilogue that he himself could have contrived to win the approbation of literary critics by making the events in his novel turn out in the end to be only a bad dream that marked a night for one of the principal characters:

> The reader who relishes happy stories would be reassured; the ideological fighter who calls for plain truth would all of a sudden take to dreaming, forgetting for a while his preference for committed literature.
>
> But the author, as usual, preferred to scorn the gay but remorse-strewn paths of success as well as the adulterated pleasures of literary demagoguery.
> (*Deux mères*, p. 200)

Mongo Beti would thus have his readers believe that it was his stance as a politically committed writer that made him elect to present in *Les Deux Mères* an African child in a society which is as infernal as the society of Camara Laye's African child is paradisiac. The fact that Laye's novel appeared during the colonial era while his own novel is set in an independent French-speaking African country is of no importance from Beti's point of view, for the Cameroonian has always expressed the view that the French-speaking countries of black Africa have not won any real independence, that France continues to wield real power in those territories through corrupt and dictatorial African regimes protected by it.

It seems to me, however, that, fiction being what it is, Mongo Beti was able to create for Guillaume Ismaël Dzewatama a situation which is, in the final analysis, not less idealistic than the one which Camara Laye created for his African child. In real life, what would generally be more traumatic for an African child than that his black father who has married a white woman while he is away in Europe should repudiate his black wife, that is to say the child's own mother, so as to make room for the white wife? That is exactly what the father of Mongo Beti's

African child does. Here is how the novelist himself summarizes the reaction of Guillaume Ismaël to the replacement of his mother in no 28 (1982) of *Peuples Noirs – Peuples Africains* during his serialization of the story in the journal:

> In spite of the repudiation of his mother, Guillaume Ismaël, a little African, is without ill feeling towards his father's new wife, a French woman . . . . Contrary to all expectations, a great friendship develops between the black adolescent and the young white woman, who is already the mother of a mulatto baby. (p. 96)

To lend plausibility to the incongruity of the replacement of the black Agathe with the white Marie-Pierre turning out to be gratifying and beneficial to Guillaume Ismaël, the black novelist endows the blonde white woman with insuperably endearing qualities. From the moment she sets eyes on Guillaume Ismaël, Marie-Pierre conceives for the black child as much maternal affection as she has for her own mulatto baby boy even though she is, for a long time, at first led to believe that he is her black husband's nephew and not his son. When she accidentally discovers the trickery whereby she has all along been made to take Guillaume Ismaël for Jean-François's nephew, the very good-natured woman, who is of course immune to the proverbial antipathy of step-mothers to their husband's children by other marriages, not only readily forgives her black husband's deceits but also, if anything, deepens her affection for the black boy.

The title of the 1982 novel, which could be translated into English as 'The Two Mothers of Guillaume Ismaël Dzewatama', indicates clearly enough the maternal role which the novelist attributes to the white woman vis-à-vis the African child. The joint motherhood of the black Agathe and the white Marie-Pierre could even be considered as having been ultimately reduced to an undivided motherhood in favour of the white Marie-Pierre if the biological contribution of the black woman were to be discounted. Towards the end of the story, while waiting to be arrested following the discovery of a coup plot in which he has played a part, Jean-François entreats his white wife not to fail to take Guillaume Ismaël with her if she goes back to France after his arrest:

> 'If an expulsion order is issued against you and your consulate, as is usual, offers you an air-ticket, don't necessarily say no, and do consider that it will be necessary for you to buy one also for Guillaume, of whom I am going to entrust the guardianship to you definitively in due form. He will become an orphan, or almost one, if you abandon him, for his mother is no longer his mother.'
> 'How so?' asked Marie-Pierre astonished.
> 'She has recently had a child, but with my brother. I didn't tell you?'
> 'Not at all.' (*Deux mères*, pp. 198–9)

The repudiated black mother of Mongo Beti's African child thus consummates her surrender of her husband to a white woman by accepting another husband, albeit the repudiator's brother; and her repudiation and remarriage are given moral consecration by her bearing a child to her new husband.

Marie-Pierre does take Guillaume Ismaël with her when, in the 1984 sequel to *Les Deux Mères*, she returns to her country several months after Jean-François's arrest – temporarily as it turns out, and as she hoped – with the principal aim of arousing French public opinion against the iniquitous regime of the francophone African country where her black husband and many other political prisoners are languishing in a notorious detention camp. As one might expect from the superlatively good white woman, before going off to France with Guillaume Ismaël, Marie-Pierre takes the trouble to make the long trip from the country's capital to her husband's village of birth to obtain permission from the biological mother and others to take the teenage boy with her, and to say goodbye, or rather *au revoir*, to the peasants.[5]

In Camara Laye's book the African mother tries her best to prevent her son from being sent to the land of the whites for further education. Indignantly she observes:

> Every day there's some mad scheme to take my son away from me! ... Do they imagine I'm going to live my whole life apart from my son? Die with him away? Have they no mothers, those people? But they can't have mothers, of course. They would not have gone so far away from home if they'd had mothers. (*African Child*, p. 155)

In Mongo Beti's *La Revanche*, the African mother and other women at the hamlet are elated at the proposed expatriation of Guillaume Ismaël to the land of the whites under the dependable protection of his white stepmother. On making the request to take the boy away with her to her own country before the assembled women of the hamlet, Marie-Pierre

> had expected a storm of protests, outraged hecklings, perhaps a manhandling to punish her for an attempt to kidnap a child. But Guillaume wore a beatific smile. His mother and grandmother covered him with looks that radiated the pride and satisfaction that are inspired by infant prodigies.
>
> (*Revanche*, p. 131)

The ultimate point in the almost mawkish idealism whereby Mongo Beti conceives a white woman who is so good as to be loved even by the black woman she has done out of a husband is perhaps reached at the episode of *La Revanche* where, at the Special Mixed Brigade post where crowds of people are trying to hand in some food and clothing to detained relatives, Agathe spontaneously rushes into a fierce physical fight with a woman who has assaulted Marie-Pierre. (p. 31)

In a note introducing the last instalment of the serialization of *La Revanche de Guillaume Ismaël Dzewatama* in no 38 (1984) of *Peuples Noirs – Peuples Africains*, the Cameroonian author indicated that the novel was 'second of a series that will therefore continue' (p. 113). One

cannot of course tell the form which the writer will give to future
Dzewatama novels if he ever does produce such subsequent volumes
after a break of over ten years. What can be said on the strength of the
two volumes that have appeared is that the novelist ended up not being
faithful to the disdain he professed for happy endings at the end of the
first volume. On his arrival in France with his white stepmother
Guillaume Ismaël, among other things, receives some training in soccer
playing from a coach who is a friend of Marie-Pierre's brother. When
pressure from agents of the home regime results in his being returned to
his African country some time later, he eventually becomes such an
asset to the national team that he is able successfully to pose as a
condition for his taking part in a difficult international match in which
national honour is at stake – the release of his father and other political
prisoners from detention. On getting the news of her black husband's
release Marie-Pierre returns to Africa – definitively – to rejoin him and
Guillaume Ismaël. One could hardly imagine a happier ending.

An examination of his treatment of African childhood in the last two of
his nine novels shows that, contrary to appearances, Mongo Beti makes
use of procedures which he condemned in Camara Laye's treatment of
the theme in his first novel. The lesson from that is, perhaps, that
literary criticism should be approached with a spirit of tolerance even
by talented creative writers. It would be much better, and no doubt more
correct, to say that the fact that white womanhood is somewhat
apotheosized in the person of Marie-Pierre in the two Dzewatama
novels indicates that the outspoken African nationalist that Mongo Beti
is known to be does not confuse anti-imperialism with anti-white
racism than to suspect the Cameroonian novelist, (who after all has
lived longer in France than in his own country) of buttering up the
white race with a view to making money from a large readership.

It is also to be noted, incidentally, that in the two Dzewatama novels
the Cameroonian author betrays particular affection for a character who
is even more of a child than Guillaume Ismaël, namely Jean-Paul, the
mulatto baby boy of the black Jean-François Dzewatama and the blonde
Marie-Pierre, who is, however, of secondary importance in the stories.
This obvious acceptance of union of the black and white races which
the mulatto child symbolizes would encourage me still further in my
opinion that Mongo Beti and the late Camara Laye, whom people are
wont to consider to be ideologically incompatible, have both, in their
treatment of the theme of childhood, ultimately written in advocacy of
the brotherhood of man.

## NOTES

1. In this study, I shall make quotations from published English translations of the studied French texts whenever such published translations were available to me, as was the case for *The African Child* and *The Poor Christ of Bomba*. The editions of the published English translations used will of course be shown in the list of works cited.
2. It is to be recalled that Mongo Beti's first novel, *Ville cruelle*, for which there does not seem to exist a published English translation, appeared in 1954 under the pseudonym of Eza Boto.
3. *Remember Ruben*, Mongo Beti's, 1974 novel begins with the hero, Mor-Zamba, as a child, or rather as an adolescent; but far more attention is given to the hero's adult years than to his childhood.
     I have not yet seen published English translations of *Les Deux Mères* and *La Revanche*. My quotations in English from these two books will therefore be my own translations from the French originals. Similarly, quotations in English from journal articles by Mongo Beti will be my own translations.
4. The first instalment of the serialization, which appeared in 20 (1981): 152–89 of the journal with the subsequently abandoned title gave the name of the child as Guillaume Henri Joseph, and that of the child's mother as Raymonde. A note introducing the second instalment, which appeared in 25 (1982): 124–49 of the journal pointed out the title change and the renaming of the child and its mother as Guillaume Ismaël and Agathe respectively. The changing of the two names was evidently due to the novelist's wish to include Protestantism, in addition to Roman Catholicism, in his African child's background.
5. That was the white woman's second visit to her black husband's village of birth. During the first visit, she had, among other things, personally taken part in the village women's back-breaking labour with rudimentary farming tools.

## WORKS CITED

A. B. (Alexandre Biyidi). 'L'Enfant noir'. *Présence Africaine* 16 (Special issues series) (1954): 419–22.
Beti, Mongo. 'Les Deux Mères de Guillaume Ismaël Dzewatama'. *Peuples Noirs – Peuples Africains* 28 (1982): 96–126.
——. *Les Deux Mères de Guillaume Ismaël Dzewatama, futur camionneur*. Paris: Buchet/Chastel, 1982.
——. 'L'Enfance précaire et cahoteuse de Guillaume Dzewatama'. *Peuples Noirs – Peuples Africains* 20 (1981): 152–89.
——. *La Revanche de Guillaume Ismaël Dzewatama*. Paris: Buchet/Chastel, 1984.
——. *The Poor Christ of Bomba*. Trans. Gerald Moore. London: Heinemann Educational Books, 1971. Trans. of *Le Pauvre Christ de Bomba*. Paris: Laffont, 1956.
——. (See A. B.).
Laye, Camara. *The African Child*. Trans. James Kirkup. Glasgow: Fontana Books, 1959. Trans. of *L'Enfant noir*. Paris: Plon, 1953.
——. *A Dream of Africa*. Trans. James Kirkup. Glasgow: Fontana Books, 1970. Trans. of *Dramouss*. Paris: Plon, 1966.

---

## Absence of Conflict in Maturation in *The African Child*

---

## G. N. Marete

Since many positive things have been said in praise of *The African Child* as a classic handling of formative years it might help initially to approach the work from a different perspective. Of central concern are the novel's structural deficiencies and how they combine, not in order to make a hash of Camara Laye's fictive craft but to deny the work touches of excellence in presenting childhood experience. In a way, some of these faults result from justifiable choices.

To suppose that a work of art can attain to sublimity by eliminating as prime an element of the narrative contract as tension is a presupposition that assumes that this structural requirement can be substituted. And yet conflict out of which tension emanates is the mainstay of literary composition. When Adele King notes that the work proceeds without fulfilling this fundamental of the narrative engagement,[1] it is not to expostulate on its dispensability. What is involved in this approach on Laye's part is not falsification of experience but rather a reduction of what constitutes it by his selection of material and treatment of it.

From the way the novel begins with a potentially deleterious relationship between the autobiographical narrator and the snake poised to strike, it seems as though sufficient conflict will be generated to carry the action of the novel through. But the circularity of the first chapter ends up with a pair of juxtaposed reptiles, each exemplifying what they symbolize. Although the juxtaposition blends artistically, its object is not to introduce a central conflict or to support one but rather to background the presentation of the nostalgic content of the work which seems to be one of the narrative's central concerns. The narrator laments the disruption of continuity that has made him unable to continue the dialogue with the snake begun by his lineage in time immemorial: 'Yes it was like a conversation. Would I too converse like that one day? No: I was still attending the school' (p. 21)[2]

What the opponents of negritudist literature[3] object to is this tone of regret, for instance, about being still in school as though this autobiographical narrator should have been left alone by the movement of

91

history to carry out dialogues with benevolent serpents when what is needed is a more vigorous acceptance of the inevitability of change in the given circumstances. The narrative unfolds primarily through contrastive juxtapositions with chapter one introducing a contrastive method that places the harmful snake and the harmless counterpart reptile of the workshop side by side.

In the new configuration of symbols, the flame of the workshop is contrasted with the fire of the railway engine. But whereas the former is harnessed to the fundamental needs of the community such as the smelting of gold, the latter is depicted as a devastating force. One cannot fail to notice the reluctance to fully integrate the railway into the communicational activities of a people who cannot escape coming to terms with it. Yet what leaves an indelible imprint on the mind of the boy growing up is not the services rendered by the railway but the suspicions that its presence is a danger. It seems as though the young narrator disparages the engine (p. 14) in favour of the forge (p. 32) for when the former is described, it is in terms of 'causing fires, frights, and possibly attracting in the strangest manner deleterious serpents into the compound' (p. 15). The economic value of the track appears hurriedly described as the narrator hurries off to the enthralling spectacle of the workshop.

Where the railway is depicted in African literature in novels such as Ngugi's *A Grain of Wheat* or Sembene Ousmane's *God's Bits of Wood*, there is no attempt to dismiss it in this peculiar manner. In Sembene's novel, for instance, what is irksome is not the presence of a mechanized mode of communication but the reduction of labour to something almost tantamount to this mechanization. And this forms part of the rationale for the strike. In Ngugi's novel, the railway forms part of the background against which characters undertake their leisure, for not being workers there, they find the train's arrival a refreshing event to witness. Even in *The River Between* where Ngugi first portrays the railway as the iron snake prophesied to come, what is criticized is infringement of land ownership, not the railway itself.[4]

Thus in *The African Child*, the presence of the railway appears like the violation of the inviolable landscape in which the setting of the text is placed. This idyllic retreat into nature as though machines are to be eschewed is typical of the way the work at first handles alien elements that have not been fully integrated into the cultural milieu the author presents. The emergence of the modern city represented by Kourassa offers a proof for this assertion. The narrator's initial dismissal of Kourassa in favour of Tindican suits the parabolic mode of the text. Tindican being the rural idyllic where grandmothers possess the paradoxical secret of youthful vigour (p. 33) is endorsed as a more attractive alternative than the town where the railway engine sets compounds and fences on fire. The implication is that the railway passengers seem to be uncomfortable travellers out to nowhere, condemned to witnessing fences on fire left behind by their chosen means of travel, while it becomes the narrator's sole monopoly to a meaningful journey on foot to the paradisiacal retreat where grandmothers never age. The narrative, true to its contrastive juxtapositions invites the reader initially to ignore Kourassa as inferior to the ritual world of Tindican where the communal ethos and the spirit of nature prevail, with the touch of nature permeating human relations and seasonal tasks.

Yet with all the admiration of the communal reality at work, there remains the question of whether the city is not a 'necessary evil'. When the text eventually comes round to making the point, it is not because the antipathy between the rural and the urban is rendered inoperable. The autobiographical profile the narrative is meant to follow forces the text to accept modern communication since the narrator cannot link up with the growing metropolis of his country on foot.

But this does not eliminate the implied polarity between the urban and the rural since both are still presented on the plane of mutual exclusiveness. Their irreconcilability is conceded easily but the missing statement about their necessary co-existence is a different matter. It is not forthcoming because the narrative scheme of the work is not meant to highlight the ambivalences that characterize modernity on the continent. The resilience of human potential that derives from homogeneity in cultural responses as exemplified by Tindican is the narrative's central concern. As Adele King points out this is carried out to the extent where 'too much individual excellence is considered impolite'.[5] Thus Uncle Lansana cannot outreap other reapers in spite of his high speed.

The work's concern is harmonization of the past so that what cannot harmonize easily is invariably presented as contradictory to that past; hence the text's preference for features that highlight contrariness. The young narrator's own education is subject to the general principle of contraposition that operates throughout the text. As mentioned earlier the narrator observes nostalgically that since he is still in school, he cannot partake of the events at the workshop (p. 2) which he tries to catch up with at night from apprentices. Here again, what is highlighted is not the workshop as the traditional equivalent of school for apprentices preparing for an occupation; the crucial issue as the narrator sees it is the way school denies him the privilege of becoming part of the ritual that forges ore into valuable items for purposes like ornamentation.

A disparity between traditional formal education and modern career preparation is insisted upon so that initially what the reader witnesses is not a society willingly making a transition and adapting itself to modernity. Transition to a large extent implies discontinuity and the discontinuity is what the work is about – the break between the work-shop ritual for which life had prepared him and the inevitability of another career. This aspect of the book like its other concerns does not reflect a confluence of cultures with a possibility of coalescence. Neither is there a linkage between the old and the new. Incorporating the old elements into the new or vice versa seems either a contradiction or is too exacting for any meaningful threading to take place. Certain constraints operate to make total cohesion possible only at the theoretical level.

But even here, the treatment of non-indigenous elements presents a challenge to the author who seems torn between the contrapositions he presents. He manages to control his medium so that absolute polarities and anathematizations of everything alien do not become constitutive. Nevertheless, its not being formative in the development of theme and character does not mean that certain reservations about the new institutions coming into being in the transition to modernity do not become noticeable. Part of the reason for the narrative's avoidance of conflict as a means to generating suspense is the concern to preserve the past in an entirely pure form. But no suggestion is being made here to the effect that the text is a subjective namby-pamby depiction of pre-colonial times for even if a narrator is objective he cannot as Wayne Booth has remarked 'be neutral to all values'.[6]

What is to be noticed is that no character in the traditional set-up is allowed any defect of character much worse than minute peccadilloes. But the school becomes the melting point of social evils so that the headmaster and the boys as we see them through juvenile eyes appear the embodiment of all the distasteful things which a recollection of childhood could consider worthy of fictionalization. All this time the narrative has avoided the structural requirement of mystification of plot for the generation of tension and suspense since the conflicts of traditional society and the denouement these would require might cast doubts on a past that must be presented as unexceptionable.

But now that a non-indigenous institution is becoming the focus of the narrative, it must be targeted as the hideout of insidious bullies since all the boys who roam the idyllic countryside must be portrayed honorifically. The episodes involving the bully and the headmaster carry some of the most intense tension in the text in addition to generating suspense rather than following the narrative's practice of simply juxtaposing symbols. Since hardly any other character outside the school is depicted in such bleak terms as the headmaster and the bully, the assumption on which the narrative proceeds is that the institution makes them.

Yet it is not possible to look at the society in question and accept without reservation the supposition that everyone is punctilious until the new modes of social organization appear to cause all the misery at school which the young narrator has to endure. The claims of cultural wholesomeness in an untinted integrated form until alien elements arrive, seems an overstatement which the text cannot substantiate. This mystification of content appears most patently manifested in the portrayal of the characters in the narrative.

Given that in Barthian terms a work's units often need to 'constitute an enigma and lead to its solution'[7] the choice is really between mystification of plot, with promises of disclosure or mystification of content at the expense of structural considerations. Lack of structural mystification by postulation of conflict is what the narrative scheme opts for. But it is not an option that costs it nothing, the main lost opportunity being what Jean Piaget considers the transformational aspect of structure.[8] One thing that cannot be an ingredient or result of conflict is stasisness. By presenting a society without conflict, Laye loses out on exemplifying the transformational process that renews society. Once conflict is excluded from a narrative strategy, transformation of elements that constitute the story is forfeited since formations and transformations at any level cannot be mapped out in the denouement. Characters (except the narrator), landscape and the entire world of the novel remain almost static.

Instances of this stasisness can be seen in the way the parents of the narrator are presented. Being punctilious beyond improvement they embody the principles of parenthood. Before anything else is said, it must be recognized that the narrator by choosing an autobiographical line centred on childhood has hardly any choice concerning the omission or inclusion of parents. Another variable in this complex area of selection of material is what an African child can say about his parents given the delicate nature of this relationship. Thus apart from the general absence of conflict in the novel, parents in a childhood novel in these circumstances can only enter into those relationships that the child understands or those things about the privacy of the home that can be made public.

If a main reason is sought for showing a parent in combative context in *The African Child* it must be to understand the protectiveness extended to the narrator as an offspring needing it in the helpless process of maturation. The young narrator's confrontation of the bully and the school administration could be said to be almost a contradiction to the picture he would have the reader form about his punctilious father:

> My father was an open-handed, and in fact, a lavish giver; no matter who turned up, he would share meals; . . . I might have remained everlastingly hungry if my mother had not taken the precaution of putting my share on the side. (p. 14)

[a finely tailored exposition of indiscriminate generosity ('no matter who turned up') hospitality carried almost to harmful extremes. Is one to assume that if the bully turned up, he would receive this hospitality? The picture of a father who receives such encomiums ending up in a physical combat seems incongruous unless one is prepared to accept the observation sometimes expostulated about human beings exhibiting contradictory traits of character. When a man who is prepared to partly starve himself for his visitors to be well fed suddenly flares up and engages in physical combat his behaviour seems out of character. But the narrator sees him as the model father and to some extent the contradiction is not so outrageous when the parental protective instinct is under gross provocation. Even then, physical assault by this model father seems like an introduction from the cliffhanger episode in a work where the author has suddenly realized that conflict, tension, combat, confrontation and assault can constitute a favourable set of parameters by which the work's meaning and achievement may be judged.]

No serious tension is generated at home. The father being generous to the point of keeping the narrator 'everlastingly' starved (p. 14), it becomes the mother's duty to take the precautions of maintaining in the home the balance between generosity and potential squandering. The mother is the principle of proportion itself and she is re-created to mediate those qualities of femininity that check goodness from becoming deleterious. But the narrative suggests that she has success only when it comes to preserving comestibles but not anywhere else: 'I have less than others, since I give everything away; and would even give away the last thing I had, the shirt on my back', (p. 19). Thus apart from her parental obligations, the narrator's mother's duty is to safeguard against harmful benignity. And since the novel is not about conflicts, there cannot be a resolution for this potentially pauperizing problem raised in the text.

Since the book's concern is not to spell out plot complications as a paradigm from where to radically transform situation and character in the proposed denouement, the question one asks at the beginning seems to be the same at the end – that is what happens to the African child? Other questions do not seem very relevant because this is a work in which there is hardly anybody else worth following up through the story except the young protagonist himself. He has no permanent antagonist to contend with except the problem of maturation – if this process could be personified in this manner.

In the absence of a permanent antagonist to confront, the text can do little else with its hero but to proceed by augmentation of rites of passage which the narrator must undergo to mature. The proliferations of context and situation that antagonistic action could engender, as is certainly evidenced by the temporary appearance of the bully, is not forthcoming due to the elimination of permanent antagonism. The upsurge of action and the intensification of tension that would be present in a conflict-ridden text cannot be expected in a work like *The*

*African Child.* The treatment of action is almost linear with hardly any mountains to climb. Its confinement to this horizontal plane does not, however, mean that one encounters nothing that can be considered an uprush providing variety to the linearly ordered action. When rites of passage such as the Konden Diara initiation ceremony are introduced, the event takes the structural role of an antagonist and the action momentarily becomes anabatic.

But the anabatic action is conceived in formative not transformative terms. The envisaged end result is the increase of courage in the process of maturation rather than transformation of character by an experience too profound to preserve the original identity intact. The work is not concerned with the formation of a new identity. If anything, the opposite is true since the formative principle in the text is geared towards exemplifying how one attains a mature equilibrium within his culture, an identity that cannot be supplemented by any other kind of experience.

An experience profound enough to become transformational is the confinement for the purpose of incision and maturation into men. Here, the personal identity attained within the cultural milieu is reflected by the gift of a new hut that defines the initiate as mature and capable of ordering his own affairs. A new hut and new set of clothes define the emergent personality somewhat transformed into an adult by the experience of circumcision. But this transformation is not a change of the original self into something beyond the culture itself. Cultural identity and conformity must be retained regardless of the forces that might threaten to supplant it.

There is plenty of evidence in the text that the marks of the new identity do not define the individual outside the culture. The narrator's mother still has immense control of the young adult who could easily be victim in the casuistry regarding morality. Admission is made that the boy has become an adult but focus is drawn to the fact that the adult is *young* and lacks experience in the climacteric time of maturation. In reserving the right to determine the company the young adult should keep and the duration of such social contacts, the mother does not see herself as contradicting the conferment of adulthood on the new adult the home has produced.

The narrator then as an African child is not growing up in a society where graduation into adulthood is marked by attainment of a certain number of years after which a licence that could be used licentiously is issued. Apart from the bully episode, this is one of the two other areas of serious potential conflict in the text, the mother poised to play an antagonistic role in the enforcement of prohibitions. All that needs to happen is for the narrator to throw cares to the wind and insist on lengthening the duration of the son's social contact even without becoming licentious – and a heated conflict ensues. But the narrator portrays himself as representative of the practice of conforming. Had he depicted an exception to general conformity, the story would have at this point imbibed an element of conflict spiralling the action upward.[9]

Such conflict might not have been normative for the African childhood experience but it would have presented an exceptional case that some might have preferred. This also raises an essential question on how autobiography may be written. In the fictionalization of a true experience, the writer is not allowed to invent. In other words, to what extent should the 'I' of other forms of verbal art be considered synonymous to the 'I' of the autobiographical narrative?[10]

More appropriately to the concerns of this work, to what extent is the 'I' of *The African Child*, the Camara Laye of real life? It is not easy to assume that in the telling of the tale the first-person narrator who speaks in the text is the same all the time. In the first place, the young narrator about to be bitten by a snake in chapter one is not the 'same' narrator at the end of the text. His perceptions have been modified by his experiences, one of which has made him decide to forget the forge in search of its modern equivalent abroad. Furthermore, the narrator engaged in the craft of fiction overseas, re-creating his experiences back home is a much more mature person than the other two.

If this is the case, the conflict in the text is internal in the narrator rather than external. The work is about coming to terms with one's divided selves and reaching a reasonable compromise. One reason the personal tensions are not conspicuous is because the narrator is too young for them to acquire dramatic quality.[11] Furthermore the work does not permit sustained opening of the narrator's mind during the reminiscences he recounts to give the reader sufficient appreciation of the problems of adjustment.

As a person dissenting with his own opinions, the narrator chooses not to dramatize this discord. Initial equivocation with regard to where he should end up in his career is committed to the passage of time which eventually solves the problem for him. On occasions, however, the conflicts get translated into serious dialogues that border on verbal confrontations. The narrator proposes to return home to Kouroussa rather than pursue a defective form of education, a proposal full of dramatic tension. In this dialogue with his uncle, he almost locates an antagonist to contend with. But the uncle is ready with an answer before tension can build up to explosive proportions.

The work is not about the inadequacies of the kinship system in coping with eventualities but rather the efficacy of the members in diffusing potential explosions. The narrator's uncle is able to mediate in a difficult situation. Someone else might have given the same advice he extends to his nephew but it might have fallen on deaf ears. In Levi-Strauss's words, a kinship system is part of a co-ordinated mechanism 'the function of which is to insure the permanency of the social group by means of intertwining consanguineous and affinal ties'.[12]

Thus part of the reason why external conflict in the text is precluded is because the childhood experiences are meant to demonstrate how efficacious the social milieu is in meeting the needs of the maturing individual. Given this narrative requirement, subjection to social control is rendered as a positive temperament trait as means to preserving the paradigms of value spelt out by the social institutions, kinship being one such. In Viconian terms as rephrased by Terence Hawkes, human institutions operate through a universal mental language exhibiting capacity in man 'not only to formulate structures, but also to submit his own nature to the demands of their structuring'.[13]

If an individual is not at variance with the social institutions of his own culture, the fiction in which this happens might seem peculiar to one used to the Western novel whose fundamental premise is to reflect individuated beings in conflict with the social set-up that limits the pursuance of their interests. But here what is witnessed is conformity to the structuring of the social context as an important requirement for the formation of a mature self. Absence of conflict denies the reader ding-dong contexts but authenticates the institutions that produce the narrator and the meaning that his narrative contract requires him to communicate.

But submission to the kinship system is not the only criterion for reaching maturation since, as noted earlier, other institutions like Konden Diara exist to reinforce the mores that perpetuated gallantry. In this situation fear has to be artificially produced and then surmounted by initiates who have no idea that the lionized noise is artificial. Apart from reinforcing traits of gallantry this seems to be part of the wider scheme of totemic logic that operates in the text to enable characters to confront the hostile environment by reference to their guardian totems.

To speak of totemic logic might seem like a contradiction in terms since the idea of appropriating totems could be said to be more instinctual than rational. But this would only be so if totems are considered as a separate mental language different from other aspects of the language by which the social institutions in this community are created. More careful scrutiny of the relational aspects of those institutions would reveal the fact that the dissimilitude is only apparent. Totemic conceptualization of experience would have its foundations in some mythology, functional or obsolete, for in mythology there is a converging pattern of logical wholeness that would authenticate the institutions in the text. Although no explicit mythology is presented in *The African Child*, it is not possible to dismiss the possibility of there being a mythology extant or obsolete behind the totems presented in the text.[15]

But the main question in this reading is conflict and not mythology. Perhaps the most potentially explosive episode is when the young narrator decides that he is going overseas, a matter his mother turns out to be most apprehensive about. There is a pattern of repetition about the mother nearly assuming an antagonistic stance in matters only for the issues in question to be resolved in some way. What makes this one different is that it involves sacrifice that seems impossible for the kind of mother the text has presented to make. The imperative of taking up the opportunity has been so forcefully backgrounded that the narrator at this point depicts it with the impetus of an inevitability.

The father has been long reconciled to the fact that his son cannot make his occupation the ritual production of artifacts where cantillations are as important as designing and fashioning out auriferous ornaments. The situation is potentially tempestuous. The narrator has yielded to the impulsion that has moved him from his roots to meet the challenges of a wider world. But the dynamics of this movement stand poised to be halted by a mother whose perception of the world is in terms of kinship. Committing a son to his uncle is not tantamount to giving him licence to roam the world.

At one level the action is spontaneous, at least in the narrator's desire to depart. Yet it is not simply a matter of packing and saying goodbye. That is why on the mother's part, the matter is initially subjected to an interesting tentativeness. This does not proceed from the failure to comprehend the issues at stake but rather from the risk of letting a young adult take charge of his own affairs; hence the mother finds it impossible to resist. She can only hesitate. Certificates have begun to replace the rites of passage. *The African Child* depicts and no matter what or how nostalgically the author makes his narrator look at the matter, some of the changes he is apprehensive about are irreversible. When he returns, he might find the round hut described at the beginning of the text as 'proudly helmeted with the thatch' (p. 12) has to be replaced by the 'zinc' houses of Achebe's novels. The implication at the social level is that what Ravenscroft calls 'the search for new concepts of community' is inevitable.[16]

---

## NOTES

1. Adele King, *The Writings of Camara Laye*, see p. 20.
2. Camara Laye, *The African Child*, c. 1954 trans. James Kirkup (Glasgow: Collins, 1987). All other references refer to this edition.
3. See Fredrick Case's article on objections to negritude as a Utopian approach to African experience in *African Literature Today*. 7 (1975): 65–75.
4. Bernth Lindfors in WLWE 20 (1) 1981 p. 28 refers to Ngugi's article 'African Culture: The mistake that Kenyatta Made', an attack on *Facing Mount Kenya* as a work that looked at the past 'through a distorted mirror of an ideal African Culture now lost, but which should be revived'. The article is subtitled 'There's no going back to the past.'

5. King: 20.
6. See in Wayne Booth's *The Rhetoric of Fiction* the article titled 'General Rules, II: All authors should be objective', pp. 67–88. Also Norman Simms identifies the oral traditions in an article titled 'Rights of Passage' as posing the challenge of integration to the narrative technique. These oral traditions of the narrative carry inescapable values to which the writer cannot be entirely neutral all the time.
7. Roland Barthes, quoted by Terence Hawkes in *Structuralism and Semiotics*, p. 116.
8. Jean Piaget cited by Hawkes: 16.
9. In a work like *The River Between* where the hero incorporates an element of dissent against his culture, he opts to plan marriage from the wrong side, which generates a lot of tension.
10. The form to consider here is the lyric or song form such as Okot p' Bitek's *Song of Lawino*.
11. One main problem dramaturgy has to face is the fact that children are excluded from the central action as main characters by constraints of performance.
12. Levi-Strauss quoted by Hawkes: 38.
13. Giambattista Vico's idea as extended by Hawkes: 15.
14. Fernando Lloyd has an article in which a Tasaday proverb expresses the kinship system as 'Let us call all men one man'. See the article in *Awakened Conscience: Studies in Commonwealth Literature*.
15. See Northrop Frye's article. 'Myth, Fiction and Displacement', in *Literary Criticism* (Ed. Trilling) where he argues that a poet or novelist may work in areas of human life apparently remote from the shadowy gods and gigantic story outlines of mythology, p. 585 The key word here is *apparently* since in *The African Child* myth is apparently absent.
16. *World Literature Written in English* 1984, p. 260.

# WORKS CITED

Bernth, Lindfors. 'Ngugi wa Thiongo's Early Journalism', *World Literature Written in English* 20 (1) 1981.

Booth, Wayne. *The Rhetoric of Fiction*. Chicago: University of Chicago Press, 1966.

Case, Fredrick, 'Negritude and Utopianism,' *African Literature Today* 7, 1975.

Fernando, Lloyd, 'A Note from the Third World towards the Redefinition of Culture'. In *Awakened Conscience: Studies in Commonwealth Literature*, Ed. C. D. Narasimhaiah, New Delhi: Sterling Publishers, 1978.

Frye, Northrop. 'Myth, Fiction and Displacement'. In *Literary Criticism: An Introductory Reader*, Ed. Lionel Trilling. New York: Holt, Rinehart and Winston, 1970.

——. *Anatomy of Criticism*. Princeton: Princeton University Press, 1957.

Gikandi, Simon. *Reading the African Novel*. Nairobi: Heinemann; London: James Currey, 1987.

Hawkes, Terence. *Structuralism and Semiotics*. London: Routledge, 1989.

Ravenscroft, Arthur. 'Third World Literature: Purpose of Indulgence'. In *World Literature Written in English* 23.1 (1984).

Simms, Norman. 'The Essential Contradiction'. In *Silence and Invisibility. A Study of the Literatures of the Pacific, Australia, and New Zealand*. Washington D.C.: Three Continents, 1988.

Lekan Oyegoke

The theme of childhood has gained in importance in African writing since the appearance of Camara Laye's *The African Child* and, latterly, Wole Soyinka's *Aké: The Years of Childhood*. The unusual plight of the child in Africa would appear to have spawned a number of interesting new titles whose materials and structures obey an organizing principle which either targets young readership or examines the experience of childhood, or does both. It seems though that the child motif is central in literature to capturing and retaining both the interest and the attention of the young reader.

An index of this development, literary interest in the child or children's literature, may well lie in the profile of the entries submitted for the 1995 Commonwealth Writers Prize.[1] Of the total number of twenty-seven works of prose fiction received in the African region, fourteen were from South Africa alone and of the fourteen, twelve examine the theme of childhood in one way or another.

That the bulk of new writing and childhood and children's literature in the last year should have come from South Africa is scarcely surprising: a new horizon of freedom and virtually unlimited opportunities has opened up for all races in South Africa with the collapse of the apartheid system of government in 1994. Furthermore, the South African economy remains the largest, most sophisticated and buoyant in Africa; whilst the economies and infrastructures in many other parts of Africa are, sadly, taking their last gasps of life, the first world infrastructure in South Africa is such that publishing and writing can only be said to be about to enter a golden age.

It is some time now since the scholar Lewis Nkosi described South African literature as rather journalistic. Assuming the observation to have been correct and, as some scholars of African literature have argued in response to Nkosi's charge, that given the historic moment of apartheid in South Africa, South African literature could not but be journalistic, political and propagandist, a new artistic canvas has now unrolled before the South African writer. Today's realities are now different from yesterday's; pre-1994 South African literature has been overtaken by change – going from protest literature and the poetics of self-assertion to the properly aesthetic in literature.

In reality and as reflected in much recent literature, the adult world may seem to have changed but in real terms the situation of the child in Africa remains largely dismal. The child, more than anyone else, is under assault from hunger, malnutrition, disease, ignorance and child abuse. Children have been conscripted to fight in wars started by adults in Angola and Mozambique, in Rwanda and Burundi, Somalia and Sudan, Liberia and Sierra Leone; in Nigeria of the 1960s children were as much victims of mindless random pogroms as adults; and scores of child soldiers have stood trial, accused of having taken part in genocide, the reckless mass killing of other unarmed children.[2]

The ironic ring of the late Ingrid Jonker's 'The Child Who Was Shot Dead by Soldiers at Nyanga' is unmistakable, viewed against the persistent traumatization and brutalization of the child all over Africa. Jonker's poem is prognostic of freedom: now attained in South Africa but threatened by some of the more intractable consequences of apartheid practices prior to the general elections in 1994. Jonker's daring poem which fittingly opened the first democratically elected parliament in South Africa is a tribute to the African child and should serve as an appropriate prologue to this essay:

The child is not dead
the child lifts his fists against his mother
who shouts Afrika! shouts the breath
of freedom and the veld
in the locations of the cordoned heart

The child lifts his fists against his father
in the march of the generations
who shout Afrika! shout the breath
of righteousness and blood
in the streets of his embattled pride

The child is not dead
not at Langa nor at Nyanga
not at Orlando nor at Sharpeville
nor at the police station at Philippi
where he lies with a bullet through his brain

The child is the dark shadow of the soldiers
on guard with rifles saracens and batons
the child is present at all assemblies and law-givings
the child peers through the windows of houses and into the hearts of mothers
this child who just wanted to play in the sun at Nyanga is everywhere
the child grown to a man treks through all Africa
the child grown into a giant journeys through the whole world

Without a pass[3]

The infamous pass in the man's hand has now been replaced by the ballot paper; but the man cannot be free if the child is still in chains. Political chains seem less virulent placed beside the more subtle and insidious psychological manacles in which the child lies entrapped.

New writing on the child should be of interest to the psychoanalytic critic. Yet, in many areas of life the psychological, the circumstantial, the familial, the sociological, the political, collaborate in complex ways in shaping the path of determinism trodden by the infant foot. The complexity of these factors is reflected in title after title of new childhood literature in Africa, ranging from the 'purely' fictional to the 'purely' autobiographical. Elana Bregin's *The Red-Haired Khumalo*[4], for example, chooses to focus realistically on how the psychological conditioning of the apartheid years is changing now rather more slowly than the overt political changes that have overtaken the country. Bregin shows, using teenage youths of different races, principally Nkululeko and Chelsea, that South Africa must look to the child and to what Jonker has described in her poem as the 'locations of the cordoned heart' for an effective removal of apartheid-bred myths and prejudices about others not of one's race. She accomplishes this task of focusing on the mind as much as on the circumstances of upbringing for lasting solutions to some of the problems of living in a multiracial society, in a manner delightfully reminiscent of E. R. Braithwaite's *To Sir With Love*, set in post second world war Britain.

On the other hand, some of the emotional and psychological consequences on the child of apartheid mysticisms, plots, counter-plots and intrigues inform such interesting works as Janet Smith's *Joe Cassidy and the Red Hot Cha-Cha*[5] and Diane Hofmeyer's delightful *Boikie, You Better Believe It*.[6] As apartheid had been designed to split black families and throw the children out into the street, it is hardly surprising that the sociological consequences of this pattern should engage the interest of new writing.

Jenny Robson's *Mellow Yellow*[7] follows in the picaresque tradition of *Oliver Twist* by Charles Dickens to examine how street gangs hatch out of factors imposed on children by adults: it is only chance meetings and fortuitous appearances that salvage the kids from the path of degeneracy and depravity on which the youths in William Golding's unforgettable *Lord of the Flies* find themselves. An elusive parent is the subject of the pitiable thirteen year old Mpho's search in Sandra Braude's novel of this title.[8]

The theme of childhood in predemocratic South Africa is the main link between Isaac Mogotsi's *The Alexandra Tales*[9] and *Cousins: A Memoir*[10] by Athol Fugard, otherwise the events they recount and the characters presented derive from two separate, or rather, separated worlds in the different worlds which make up South Africa. Both these works seem comparable, although the one is fictional and the other autobiographical. It must be acknowledged though that the deployment of the terms 'fictional' and 'autobiographical' in respect of these works is problematical. The debate as to whether there is such a thing as pure fiction or pure autobiography has scarcely abated. James Olney aptly sums up the situation when he writes:

> In talking about autobiography, one always feels that there is a great and present danger that the subject will slip away altogether, that it will vanish into thinnest air, leaving behind the perception that there is no such creature as autobiography and that there never has been – that there is no way to bring autobiography to heel as a literary genre with its own proper form, terminology, and observances. On the other hand, if autobiography fails to entice the critic into the folly of doubting or denying its very existence, then there arises the opposite temptation (or perhaps it is the same temptation in a different guise) to argue not only that autobiography exists but that it alone exists – that all writing that aspires to be literature is autobiography and nothing else.[11]

Mogotsi's narrative strategy in his fictional account is autobiographical. He adopts the epistolary technique in aid of realism and sets up a fictional Philip Kota who addresses his infantile reminiscences and observations to his mother in the form of letters, exemplified by the prologue and the epilogue to the novel. Apart from this prose device, *The Alexandra Tales* is realistic, indeed naturalistic in other ways. Some of the characters and situations described recall actual people and incidents in South African history. There is, for example, what may be described as some kind of ideological resemblance between Aunt Sylvia (though she commits suicide in the novel out of frustration as the 'mother of the nation') and Winnie Mandela; similarly, the link between Teenage Kgositsile of the Black Consciousness movement in the novel and the late Steve Biko cannot be missed. More apparent naturalistic features are the references to Alexandra, Soweto, and other apartheid era landmarks.

*The Alexandra Tales* may in fact be closer to history than to fiction regardless of the narrative disguises calculated to show the contrary. It is believed that there is at least one novel in everyone, and not only that, that a first novel is often a disguised account of true experiences. The psychoanalytic distinction between 'dream-thought', 'dream-story', and 'dream-work' in an attempt to understand the creative process should be truer of the first novel, that is, than perhaps subsequent efforts. The point about the factualness of the Mogotsi novel is not meant to detract from its merit or search it for a hidden agenda, but to show that it might be generically closer to Fugard's more overtly autobiographical effort than may be assumed.

The question about the literary affinity between *The Alexandra Tales*, hereafter referred to as *Tales*, and *Cousins* may be pursued further in line with Olney's summation quoted earlier on. How much of what in

*Cousins* Fugard describes as facts is actually factual? How much is fiction? For instance, in most autobiographies, as many autobiographers would admit, character dialogue is frequently 'novelized': euphemism for 'invented'. Fugard acknowledges a hazy recollection of some of the people, facts and experiences that he tries to deal with in the memoir. Furthermore, the principle of selectivity, the decision as to what materials to include or exclude from the writing, and the choice of perspectives, are strategies that may compromise the fidelity of the biographer's material.

A famous advert for photographic materials represents photography in the following words: 'memories are made of this'. It is interesting that both Fugard and Mogotsi have an ambivalent attitude to photographs. While Fugard's attitude runs subtly through this entire memoir, Mogotsi's is a strident condemnation of photographs in favour of 'letters':

> I could have sent you various photographs which capture different stages of my life. But the weakness of pictures is that they show only the outward person. They are mute about internal growth and emotional turmoil. They can never reflect one's recesses. They do not tell the tale of one's soul and spirit. They are thus singularly unsuited for the purpose I put before myself when I set out to write these memoirs. (p. 170)

Philip's categorical denial of the usefulness of pictures is contradicted by a photo's ability to capture his Aunt Jeannette's 'finest moment': her 'intelligence', her 'relaxed beauty, absolutely in control of circum-stances', 'this Jeannette – sober, clean, confident, composed, genteel and hopeful – was the sister my father adored and loved'. These epithets refer to the figure in the picture hanging in Philip's father's house (pp. 23–4).

Fugard describes how his coming to terms with a pile of old photos is a slow and difficult process. But when he does hit it off with the pictures, the harvest is rich, not only in terms of the flood of reminis-cences which they unleash but also the new deep psychological and emotional insights which unfold. The result is a Hally, Johnnie and Garth – cousins, children, nay, characters – who spring to life in a few pages of memoir.

The portrait that emerges of Philip's mother in *Tales* is of a battered, ill-used woman who remains elusive throughout the book. Her elusive-ness is however of strategic importance as the presumed recipient of her son's letters. More time is devoted to Aunties Jeannette, Sylvia, Dipuo, and Uncle Koos, who come out nevertheless as cardboard characters. Mogotsi's adult characters typify the ne'er-do-wells of the apartheid era, given to a life of cigarettes, alcohol, sex, mental shallowness and incurable indolence, amongst other traits.

The characters in *Tales* may be clichéd, but the deployment of flat characters has its uses, as the renowned critic E. M. Forster has argued.[12] The wooden character acquires even more significance in the South African context: apartheid was a systematic attempt to caricature black people. So, the question may be asked, if this was the case, what business has a flat character in a novel by a black writer? The answers are obvious, chief amongst which is that flat characters can be used quite as effectively as round characters, as Dickens is shown to have done. Following from this, another question emerges: have the flat characters been effectively used in *Tales*?

The stereotype aunties and uncles and grandmas and single boozing, fighting, philandering parents are presented as a given in *Tales* without adequately showing that they are creations of apartheid. This is in spite of the ideological pretences: there is a mechanical after-taste to the dramatic change that comes over Uncle Koos, for instance; Koos's metamorphosis into Rev. D. J. and back to Koos is rather unrealistic. Similarly, the transformation of the highstrung Aunt Sylvia into a fire-spitting ideologue, though less surprising than Koos's transfiguration, seems to serve only one purpose: a mouthpiece for political and socio-logical formulations which, coming at this time, should make Nkosi wince. In spite of Philip's ideological propensity, he seems to be a bit fallible sometimes in his grasp of himself, other people, and some situations. His blood mother is unjustly publicly assaulted for coming for him in his father's house; the experience does not jolt him. He witnesses a scene of explicit multiple sexual orgy, his sleep is only delayed for a while, little more than that happens. He is only deeply affected when he encounters a white girl while on a visit to his grandmother at Orange Grove where she is an exploited domestic servant. The budding innocent friendship between himself and the white girl is nipped by the actions of suspicious, fearful, discriminating adults (pp. 79–80). The scenario follows a familiar pattern in hate–riven multiracial societies; it recalls the interesting sonnet 'To a White Child' by the Zimbabwean Henry Pote:

> Your mother and father, eccentrics
> And venturesome, made us friends.
> You, innocent, guileless, saw no tricks
> And always accepted my presence
> With nonchalance and little wonder.
> Something about my grins won you over,
> You would constantly wait and hover
> Till opportunity turned to tell your secret naive
> About your doll, your prowess, and how you strive
> And need my aid to reconstruct a broken toy.
> Will your trust vanish when you grow older?
> It cannot be: you're already too wise
> To somersault and move anti-clockwise.[13]

Philip's obsequious grandma is so embarrassed and shaken by the discovery of the friendship between the black and white kids that she punishes Philip for it. Neither she nor her white madam cares to find out from the youngsters how in the first place the girl came to be in the servants' quarters which she had never visited before. The adult women, by their behaviour, simply conclude that Philip is the culprit, the white girl the innocent victim of his pranks:

> When I finally stopped crying, my grandma turned off the cold shower. What she could not possibly know was that when I stopped crying and she switched off the cold shower that day, I came of age. Biologically I remained a boy, but internally I matured. I ceased to expect love, tenderness and compassion. Something innocent and fragile in me died. Since that day I have always been guarded in the expression of my emotions and cautious in accepting friendly advances. (pp. 81–2)

In Freudian terms the loss of innocence which is a stage in the progression from childhood to maturity is a complicated process. Though complex, the process is often dramatic rather than cumulative, with an undercurrent of sexuality. Philip's reading of the incident involving himself, the white girl and the adults presents a problem. How correct a reading is it? Can one talk about loss of innocence without qualification? Is what Philip refers to as 'loss of innocence' typical of racial situations, slum conditions, or the general condition of the child?

Hally in *Cousins* grows up in the comparatively privileged white sector of the South African society; his loss of innocence takes place within family circles. As do Michaela, Antony, Pauline and Justin, trapped in a confidential web of incestuous relationships as children, in Alison Lowry's *Wishing on Trains*.[14] The unhappy encounter with a white girl on the part of Philip in *Tales* cannot be, in my opinion, more important than the public humiliation of his mother before his very eyes, if loss of innocence is taken in a general sense. Nor can it be weightier, in terms of thrusting maturity into a child's psyche, than watching live sexual intimacy between unmarried adults.

With old photographs serving as a mnemonic and creative catalyst, Fugard is able to probe the past and to come to a deeper understanding of the roles which different people had played consciously and unconsciously in shaping the destiny of the young Hally. The most momentous influences were from his mother and father and, more subtly, from his cousins Johnnie and Garth: Johnnie through his admirable musical talent and affable personality, and Garth through his often queer and undignified attitude to life. Fugard presents with remarkable sensitivity the impact on Hally's mind of Garth's confession of his homosexuality, a disclosure which marked for Hally the loss of innocence. Garth's childhood had been scarred by parentally induced fear and sense of insecurity.

Mogotsi's handling of a similar experience in *Tales*, that is, one involving the loss of sexual innocence, not through physical participation but through emotional and psychological exposure, is casual. All of chapter seven of *Tales* is devoted to a graphic description of sex between Koos and Jeannette and Sylvia. The effect of the spectacle on the young Philip is represented as follows:

> Not long thereafter the three fell asleep. Perhaps because of drunkenness, or perhaps because of the demanding sex session, they soon began snoring like pigs.
>
> I stayed awake for a long time, until birds started chirping to herald the new morning. (pp. 39–40)

Nothing is said about what went on in Philip's mind after the incident before he was rescued by sleep – assuming that he had a sound sleep unhaunted by memories of what he had just seen. Subsequently, the only reference to the incident is a little flashback in the following chapter: 'The memorable events described above were a remarkable conclusion to a remarkable day' (p. 41). One would have wished to have been trusted by the narrator with the specific emotive and psychological contents of the adjectives 'memorable' and 'remarkable' in those contexts. In short, what impression did the experience make on the child? Surely, there must be some link between that experience and another recorded in chapter eighteen:

> What a wonderful time it was in Bokala when Eva and I were not fighting. I laughed my lungs out when she imitated Sis Bella and Pule behind their backs. I loved our games together, when we played hide-and-seek under the table and under the beds. I enjoyed our crude jokes about each other, when we talked about the mystery of sex, when we childishly attempted sexual intercourse with each other, when we tried to unravel the mysteries of child-birth, when we secretly talked about sexual organs, when she would study my penis and I her vagina. (p. 100)

It may be helpful, therefore, in discussing these experiences to distinguish between the loss of sexual innocence and the loss of political innocence. Even so, there may not be such a thing as political innocence; what there may be is perhaps political immaturity vis-à-vis political awareness. In the ghetto conditions of township shacks the rapid psychological, and sometimes also emotional and physical, precocity of the child is guaranteed by the circumstances of want, child neglect and child abuse. The black (or indeed white) product of these conditions matures faster into alcoholism, drug addiction, premarital sex, crime and violence than into political awareness. Sometimes what is deemed political savvy in the child is no more than cover for an extension of destructive habits, the advancement of a nihilistic desire. Yet, in all of this, the child is scarcely to blame, the real culprit is the adult who created these conditions, the main offenders in South Africa being the architects of the apartheid system.

Thus what Philip calls loss of innocence after the Orange Grove experience with the white girl is actually the stirring of political consciousness, a stage in the process of growing up. The unique circumstances of apartheid ensured that the South African child attained political sophistication faster than the child elsewhere in contemporary Africa. The famous 1976 Soweto riots perhaps remain a lasting testimony to this fact, while new literature like *Tales* and *Cousins* and the others concerned with the plight of the child everywhere is a testament to the importance of the child to the humaneness and survival of the human species.

## NOTES

1. See Commonwealth Foundation press statement on 1995 Commonwealth Writers Prize.
2. See report by Louise Tunbridge entitled, 'Children Accused of Genocide in Rwanda', *Sunday Times* (South African) 17 December 1995, p. 10.
3. Es'kia Mphahlele/Helen Moffett, *Season Come to Pass: A Poetry Anthology* (Cape Town: Oxford University Press, 1994): 212–13.
4. Elana Bregin, *The Red-Haired Khumalo* (Cape Town: Maskew Miller Longman, 1994).
5. Janet Smith, *Joe Cassidy and the Red Hot Cha-Cha* (Cape Town: Maskew Miller Longman, 1994).
6. Diane Hofmeyer, *Boikie, You Better Believe It* (Cape Town: Tafelberg, 1994).
7. Jenny Robson, *Mellow Yellow* (Cape Town: Tafelberg, 1994).
8. Sandra Braude, *Mpho's Search*. (Cape Town: Oxford University Press, 1994).
9. Isaac Mogotsi, *The Alexandra Tales* (Braamfontein: Ravan Press, no date).
10. Athol Fugard, *Cousins: A Memoir* (Johannesburg: Witswatersrand University Press, 1994).
11. James Olney, *Autobiography: Essays Theoretical and Critical* (Princeton, New Jersey: Princeton University Press, 1980): 4.
12. E. M. Forster, *Aspects of the Novel* (New York: Harcourt, Brace, 1927; Harmondsworth: Penguin, 1962).
13. *Seasons Come to Pass*: 224.
14. Alison Lowry, *Wishing on Trains* (London: Mandarin Paperbacks, 1995).

Jamal Mahjoub. *In the Hour of Signs*. Oxford: Heinemann, 1996, 252 pp.

Evelyne Accad. *Wounding Words: 'A Woman's Journal in Tunisia'* (Trans. from the French by Cynthia T. Hahn). Oxford: Heinemann, 1996, 183 pp.

These two novels have more than one thing in common. They were both written by Arabic speakers (in English and French respectively). Both writers are resident in the West (Denmark and the USA) and neither would have found enthusiastic publishers in their countries of origin – Sudan and Lebanon. In this sense they are a continuation of a long Arabic tradition of search in another geographical location (or/and another language altogether) for a margin of freedom of speech that does not exist in the home country.

Jamal Mahjoub is a Sudanese–British author (in the literal sense of the words, his father is Sudanese and his mother English). He was born in England, grew up in the Sudan, and returned to England to study geology. He changed both his mind and his country of residence. *In the Hour of Signs* is his third novel. The first *Navigation of a Rainmaker*, published in 1989, showed a great deal of promise despite the fact that it fell into the now predictable formula of 'Return and Disappointment' which was perfected in Tayeb Saleh's brilliant and influential *Season of Migration to the North*. Mahjoub managed to choose his own shooting angles and demonstrated his ability to develop an independent voice. His main tool was an iconoclasm which contrasted sharply with Tayeb Saleh's more 'considerate' approach.

The same tool, honed and greatly improved, serves Mahjoub well in *In the Hour of Signs*. The readiness and ability to hit and hurt and break taboos is there. Its effect is enhanced – not reduced – by the allegorical form of the novel which is based on both Ibn Tufail's *Hai Ibn Yaghzan*, in the classical Arabic tradition, and Swift's *Gulliver's Travels*.

On one level, the novel can be read and enjoyed as an extremely well-researched 'historical documentary' work about the rise and fall of Mahdism in the Sudan. The way in which late nineteenth-century

Sudan erupted against Turco-Egyptian domination – in a twist of international power politics – involved Britain in the person and prestige of General Charles Gordon (of Khartoum) and his officers.

Chapter by chapter, in regular chronological order (broken by a single, short flash-back in chapter 30), the novel records with textbook accuracy, the signs of the rise and fall of the Mahdi, his successes in the various battles, culminating in the siege and capture of Khartoum, his death and his Khalifa's (successor's) establishment of a harsh totalitarian rule in the name of Islam. This was ended by the reconquest of the Sudan in 1898 by Lord Kitchener. The strength of the novel is its even-handedness. It depicts the brutalities of both sides in the conflict as well as the humanitarian touches displayed by the main characters. Hamilton Ellsworth, the young British intelligence officer, writes home saying that the Mahdist enemy 'is only doing what any decent fellow would, defending his country'. Gordon, besieged in Khartoum and staring death in the face, reads the Koran and says, 'The God of the Muslims is our God, Ellsworth. What I would give for a battalion of men as devoted as the Mahdi's.' The Mahdi ordered his men *not* to kill Charles Gordon; but take him prisoner. Gordon, however, was killed and the Mahdi died of natural causes. Upon reconquest of the Sudan the young British soldiers desecrated the tomb of the Mahdi and scattered his bones in the river. The successor of the Mahdi had created a police state and massacred people without a fair trial.

However, the more rewarding interpretation of the novel is the allegorical one. The Mahdi is portrayed as a man who: 'seemed to smile all the time'. This is a recognizable characteristic of Dr Hassan At-Turabi, leader of the ruling Muslim fundamentalists in Khartoum. Hawi, the Sudanese intellectual who had a liberal interpretation of the texts of Islam, returns to Sudan from his self-exile when he hears of the signs of Mahdism. He supports the revolution and, after the fall of Khartoum, is put in charge of the printing presses (inherited from the colonial administration). He sees the realities of a fundamentalist and literal application of Sharia laws. Religion is perverted in order to serve the power struggle and becomes subservient to political aspirations. He speaks out and is hanged. Hawi repeats the words of prophet Mohammed, 'Blessed are the strangers. Islam started as a stranger and it shall return as such.' These very words were the favourite maxim of the philosopher Mahmoud Mohammed Taha who was hanged for apostasy in Khartoum in 1985 at the instigation of Hassan At-Turabi. The day on which he was hanged, 18 January, has now been adopted by Arab human rights organizations as the annual Human Rights Day. The police state as well as the self-delusion which led the successor of the Mahdi to over-reach himself and provoke battles on more than one front without adequate resources is also comparable to the attitude of the ruling fanatics of today.

The general portrayal of blind fanaticism is an indication that the novel is not only about Sudan or Muslim fundamentalism but about all religious intolerance. As such it has a footprint which is much wider than the countries directly mentioned in it.

With this novel, Jamal Mahjoub enters a universal stage, far beyond the confines of nineteenth-century Sudan.

Evelyne Accad has chosen the form of a diary of a Christian Arab writer who spends a year in Tunisia and meets young women of her generation. For a time she shares their hopes and dreams. They embrace her with varying degrees of warmth generated by the common cause: greater emancipation for Arab women. They smoke cigarettes, drink wine, swim topless, talk freely about their loss of virginity and 'open relationships' in which each partner agrees to a sexual freedom that they either admit to the other or hide from them.' They even talk about orgasm. Such stuff might not raise an eyebrow in western countries; but – coming from a young woman – this is extremely explosive material in the Arab context; especially in the context of the present wave of religious resurgence which is filling the vacuum left by the failure of Arab Nationalism and the collapse of the totalitarian Socialist Alternative.

The 'diary' format makes it very easy (and enjoyable) to move from social to overtly political themes. The case for the Palestinians and for Arab nationalist aspirations is represented; the USA 'gives unconditional aid to Israel. It supports racist expansionist Zionism one hundred per cent' – as Nayla puts it. But the other point of view is also expressed in the novel. The diarist writes, 'Israel is not the only country to attack Lebanon' a clear reference to Syria. A taxi-driver says to her about Lebanon and its civil war, 'The Christians are not Arab. They should return to Europe or go to America.' She replies, 'There are Arab Christians. I'm an Arab Christian.'

There is criticism of anti-Israeli suicide bombers and a call for peaceful resistance as well as censure of the Palestinians. Moreover the 'novel' contains several 'short stories' in which women talk about their response to oppression in a male-dominated society.

In the middle of all the friendships and solidarity between women, two events stand out. When the Tunisian landlord tries to rape the diarist, his wife implores her not to report the matter to the police. As if this is not enough, some of the diarist's Tunisian friends become very cool towards her. It turns out that her links with the US Embassy (because of her grant) put her in the 'CIA suspect' category.

The most moving aspect of the novel is one which runs counter to the general feminist slant. Ahlame (whose name means 'Dreams' in Arabic) is the most liberated and provocatively emancipated of the Tunisian women. Reaching the conclusion that she can't take the backwardness and narrow mindedness of Tunisia, she goes to France, where she is confronted by racial prejudice and ends up committing suicide. This is an indication of the extent to which Arab women are not faced with a clear cut, black and white situation.

The novel contains some fascinating descriptions of ceremonies of exorcism and religious 'sufi' ceremonies, which act as traditional safety valves for the pent up frustrations of Arab women.

Men are conspicuous by their absence from the novel, except as rapists or brutal husbands. Apart from the young Palestinian lover of one of the women, men are left out. This is surprising, considering that Tunisia is the country in which a man (Habib Bourgiba – the late President) banned the veil and passed very progressive laws in favour of women's rights.

Khalid Al-Mubarak
Cambridge University, UK

Ken Saro-Wiwa. *Prisoners of Jebs*. Port Harcourt: Saros International, 1988, 180 pp.

Ken Saro-Wiwa. *Pita Dumbrok's Prison*. Port Harcourt: Saros International, 1991, 280 pp.
Distributed by African Books Collective, The Jam Factory, 27 Park End Street, Oxford, OX1 1HU.

Ken Saro-Wiwa. *Lemona's Tale*. London: Penguin, 1996, 143 pp.

Ken Saro-Wiwa. *A Month and a Day: A Detention Diary*. London: Penguin, 1995, 238 pp.

The publishing history of the four titles, two put out by Ken Saro-Wiwa's publishing house, the other two released by a major company after he had become an international figure, tells part of the extraordinary story of a most exceptional man. In the pages that follow the four books will be considered in turn, stations on the road to the scaffold at Port Harcourt, relics ensuring that Saro-Wiwa will not be forgotten. I have listed *Lemona's Tale* before the *Detention Diary* because the major part of the writing seems to have been done some time ago. As will become clear, I consider it a minor work, given international exposure by Penguin largely because of the attention focused on Saro-Wiwa by the circumstances of his execution.

Publication in book form was not envisaged when Saro-Wiwa, at the request of a journalist friend, began to write the column that eventually became *Prisoners of Jebs*. On the cover of that book, Willfried Feuser, a close observer of the Southern Nigerian scene, describes the volume as a 'breath-taking *roman-à-clef*.' He writes that it 'follows the weirdest contours of the political scene, recasting them in the mould of allegory . . . [that it] is a microcosm of Nigerian society. Like all good satire it is didactic in a distorting sort of way: an African *Mirror for Magistrates*.' As a 'come on' this is fine, conveying something of the appeal and style of the strange book. However, closer investigation leaves dissatisfaction with the description in terms of a key and an allegory. *Jebs* is altogether a more fluid work than Feuser suggests, one in which the satire and didacticism are diluted by the volume's most attractive qualities, its energy and risk – the qualities conveyed by the word 'breath-taking'.

Reading *Jebs* from beginning to end is a very different experience to that enjoyed by those who encountered the fifty-three chapters as articles in the Nigerian press. Saro-Wiwa first wrote about Jebs in *Punch* in 1977, and he returned to the conceit when he was invited to write for *Vanguard* near the end of 1985. Saro-Wiwa's column provided a commentary on events, but the style and manner were clearly evolving over the years and there are what might be described as inconsistencies or variations. Given the dangers to which the author exposed himself in writing so frankly – in the Author's Note he records that 'A number of my friends expressed grave fears for my personal safety while the instalments ran' – the disruptions are perfectly understandable. Criticism for inconsistency is valid but incurs the risk of being impertinent unless the violence of Nigerian society and the sensitivity surrounding some of the issues tackled are recognized. Saro-Wiwa's achievement lies in the eloquent writing, the creation of a fantastic and fantastical world, and the inclusion of a sophisticated, mischievous, imaginative, courageous, sometimes deeply-felt commentary.

The genesis of Saro-Wiwa's central concept is indicated in an opening paragraph that begins with eighteenth-century weight and with a tilt at a twentieth-century target (the OAU):

> In the year of our Lord nineteen hundred and eighty-five, the Organization of African Unity decided in its accustomed wisdom to set up an elite prison on the Dark Continent.

The prison, Jebs, is established on an artificial base off the coast of Nigeria: a sort of Robben Island, but one for which tenders can be invited and contracts awarded. Since the prison soon has inmates from all over Africa, Saro-Wiwa can use it and them to comment on events in a variety of countries. However, the targets of his satire, like the readers of the newspaper for which he wrote, were mostly Nigerian. After it has served as a parade ground for various follies and vices, Jebs becomes, quite literally, a target for the Nigerian armed forces – a fate, one might note, it shared with Ogoniland.

With nimble foot-work, Saro-Wiwa moves in and out, attacking his compatriots – drawing attention to swindles, scandals and frauds, to the tendency of some of his fellow countrymen to pillage, loot and plunder on a gigantic scale. With dozens of delightful turns of phrase and through the generation of bizarre and absurd situations, he provides entertainment, amusement and food for thought.

One area of bitter dispute he repeatedly exposes concerns the tactics employed by the dominant forces in the Nigerian federation. Saro-Wiwa makes repeated use of the term 'Wazobia', where 'Wa' refers through a linguistic link to the Yorubas of the West, 'Zo' to the Hausa, and 'Bia' to the Igbos (Biafrans) of the East. One of the floating satirical images through which the bullying attitude of these dominant groups is exposed is football. On the island of Jebs, a world that is sometimes parallel, sometimes tangential to Nigeria, football is, as in Nigeria, a passion. It is, however, played according to extraordinary rules, rules that are changed at Wazobian whim. The rights of Others, of minority groups within the

Federation, are constantly disregarded. The goals the Others score are not simply disallowed, they are, amazingly, credited to Wazobia! In a sense this is 'all good fun', a fantasy football match, but beneath the smile is an acerbic commentary on the manipulation of the constitution and of the federal system. Saro-Wiwa does not need to say that the Ogoni are one of the Others, an 'Out Group' constantly denied justice.

The satirical mode employed is unique, one which draws on local conventions while breaking new ground. It is flexible enough for the judge of a kangaroo court to arrive at the prison as a kangaroo (what else?), and for a real, live journalist, Pita Okute, to be transformed into 'Pita Dumbrok' who is condemned to spend most of the book suspended in a bird-cage. In these characters, precedents provided by animal fables are invoked, and yet there is a consistent concern with the contemporary. The flights of fancy are also peopled by tricksters, successful and unsuccessful. Appropriately there are references to *Basi and Company* – 'the most popular comedy on (Nigerians') television stations' (p. 121), in which Saro-Wiwa drew on trickster conventions to develop a distinctive kind of situation comedy.

Saro-Wiwa himself makes several appearances in the book and, at one point, expands on a reference to provide a revealing self-assessment of his impact as a satirist. After he has been invited to go on an 'all-expenses paid trip to Air Force Headquarters' (p. 102), Chief Popa, longterm prisoner and adviser to the Director of Jebs Prison, tells the Director that he has heard that 'Mr Saro-Wiwa has been watching this Prison for a long time,' (p. 103) and that he has been saying 'everything evil about the Prison and especially about the Nigerian inmates of the Prison'. When Dumbrok is cross-questioned about Saro-Wiwa, he replies, 'He is a mean spiteful little wretch, and so small you wouldn't find him among a colony of soldier ants. He is learning to be a satirist.' When asked what a satirist does, Dumbrok replies:

> He holds up a distorting mirror before people. Some people look into the mirror, see their reflection and get scared. (Dumbrok adds) . . . (Saro-Wiwa) spends his time picking holes in everything under the Nigerian sun: a chief's foolish cap, a thieving governor's walking stick, Customs officers' uniforms, University professors' hoods, a journalist's pen, a wrecked naval boat's deck. The Nigerians in and out of prison are sick of him. He's giving them sleepless nights.

To get a feel of the self-reflective and surrealistic nature of some of the writing, it is worth noting that the chapter moves on to an exchange between the Director and a Professor from the University of Lagos. The Professor is anxious to visit the Prison and look for 'Clichés and Verbiage'. The Director tells him, 'There are no prisoners answering such names here.' At this point a note alerts the reader to the fact that a Mr Agulanna of the Philosophy Department of the University of Lagos had accused Saro-Wiwa of writing in 'clichés and a high-sounding verbiage'. Saro-Wiwa offered him 20 naira for every cliché and every example of verbiage 'confirmed by the Professor of English at the University'. (p. 179) Saro-Wiwa's money was, incidentally, safe from

Agulanna since his writing is fresh and direct. Any clichés are firmly imprisoned within inverted commas.

The way in which recognizable individuals enter the world of Jebs Prison has been touched on in relation to Pita Dumbrok. Significantly, Saro-Wiwa allows him to listen and learn, to think and change so that a pilloried and ridiculed critic is transformed in the course of the book. A more complicated process of 'character creation' and of comment is provided by Professor, who is initially credited with profound insight into the way money might disappear. He has, we learn, an eclectic taste in music (p. 16) and a mystical link with 'professional stones'. Later in the book, he is associated with Professor in Wole Soyinka's play *The Road*: he is even given some of the lines from that play. However, despite Feuser's reference to a *roman-à-clef* and to allegory, *Prisoners of Jebs* is not the sort of book in which 'equivalences' can be established, and to complicate this issue (Professor) Wole Soyinka also makes an appearance. Indeed Soyinka arrives from Stockholm, where, shades of the Nobel Award, he has been to receive a prize, and whence he comes bearing the dynamite that, it seems, eventually destroys the island. From the presentation of Professor and of Soyinka one can appreciate Saro-Wiwa's whimsy, and obtain an impression of the sort of distorting mirror, or rather mirrors, he holds up to nature. The whimsical in *Jebs* makes it difficult to determine a coherent satirical or critical viewpoint. Saro-Wiwa was, understandably, being elusive and allusive, dodging confrontation on dangerous topics – such as secession, refusing, will-o'-the-wisp-like, to be held to account. Eventually Jebs Prison explodes, or is blown up, but this does not mean that Saro-Wiwa could not salvage material from it for more newspaper articles and, in due course, for another collection.

These were brought together to make the second book I want to consider: *Pita Dumbrok's Prison*. This volume, like its predecessor, was published by Saro-Wiwa's company, and combines a variety of themes, ideas and styles. Sometimes it is an eighteenth-century literary fable with carefully composed introductions to each chapter, sometimes a Swiftian satire, sometimes we seem to be in a world created by a politically aware Amos Tutuola, and then we are plunged into a booklet about African history. As a result, *Pita Dumbrok's Prison* can confidently be described as 'experimental', representing an attempt to come to terms with the fantastic – the imaginatively brutal, incandescently terrible, scandalously wasteful, vigorously corrupt, hugely fascinating, intriguingly creative nation that Nigeria was becoming before Saro-Wiwa's eyes.

As we make our way through the novel, now meandering, now on a roller-coaster ride, we are, as in *Jebs*, repeatedly reminded of particular events and episodes by the two-way traffic between the fantastic and the actual. In the midst of fantasy there are references to the dumping of toxic waste, the crating of a fugitive politician, the fashion for book launches, and the assassination by letter-bomb of an investigative journalist. All of which will suggest historical incidents and events to those who lived through the eighties with an eye on developments in

Nigeria. There are also comments on the way Nigeria's dominant groups (the Wazobians, of course) exploited minorities, about the way the rulers behaved and about the ease with which ordinary people abdicated responsibility. *Pita Dumbrok's Prison* is angry and witty, by turns subversive and confrontational, gently humorous and deeply engaged. Even as he launched his attacks, Saro-Wiwa must have been aware that Nigerian reality was more bizarre than his Nigerian fiction could ever be, that the wildest imaginings of the satirist were booted into the Stygian shade by the facts of Nigerian life.

On one level *Pita Dumbrok's Prison* (hereafter *Prison*) is a narrative, a sequel to *Prisoners of Jebs*, and, it seems, the second volume in a planned three-part study of Nigerian politics. Pita Dumbrok, the journalist Pita Okute mentioned above, is, in *Prison*, the lone survivor of Jebs Prison. Already far removed from Pita Okute, he moves landwards and is welcomed by the President. The journalist-survivor begins to write about the prison for the *Quarterly Messenger*, but only two instalments are allowed to appear before security forces take action. Thereafter discovering the significance, location and fate of Jebs Prison involves a number of people, and provides the main focus for the book.

In addition to Pita Dumbrok, other journalists interested in the prison are introduced. One, the beautiful Asa, goes 'underground' with Pita, and helps him produce a 'Letter' to his compatriots that provokes a popular uprising. Another is the experienced Azini and he becomes the driving force in the search to find out about, and to find, Jebs. And the third is young Biney, who finishes his National Service with a major newspaper in the course of the book and ends the story in Jebs Prison! Also caught up in the affair are Bigya, an Ishunman masquerading as a Northerner in order to advance his career in the security forces, and Ziko, the naval commander who had been given the task of blowing up the prison island but whose destructive act was, it seems, thwarted by the resourceful, powerful, mysterious Professor. Bigya and Ziko, embodiments of repressive forces, are killed in the final pages of the novel by Ita, initially an obedient member of Bigya's State Security Department, who from an involved and complicated plot, emerges as a man of action emboldened by new vision.

Restless and innovative, the novel is told from several perspectives. Many of those already mentioned narrate chapters and other voices, including that of Edward Nji, a Cameroonian who provides a fluent and detailed account of part of the background to the Jebs Affair, are introduced. As the novel moves into its stride, Saro-Wiwa dispenses with such conventions and simply shares the narrative between more storytellers, some partly characterized through their style, each drawing attention to a different facet of the situation.

As the foregoing anticipates, Jebs Prison, an enigma and a mystery (p. 56), continues in this book to provide a flexible analogy, permitting Saro-Wiwa to comment on national and international elements. We are asked, for example, to accept that the disappearing prison is tied up with Africa's financial position – it is suggested that the rescheduling of debts owed to international creditors depends on the lending nations being convinced that the 'investment' still exists.

Given Saro-Wiwa's educational background, the whole, daring, fanciful idea of a floating prison off the coast of Nigeria may conceivably have roots in classical mythology, it might be a sort of anti-Atlantis. But the island can also be associated with the worlds visited by Lemuel Gulliver and, in certain senses, it can, perhaps, be linked with existing offshore prisons, such as Robben Island and Alcatraz. Furthermore, it can, as I have already suggested, be linked with Ogoniland.

The mention of Gulliver provides a useful link when attempting to communicate the experience of reading this very unusual volume. Towards the end of the book, Azini and Biney, two latterday Lemuels, set off in a hired boat in search of Jebs. They are soon reduced to making progress in a canoe that moves under its own power and is directed by an unseen force along a particular course. They are carried to seven islands in each of which they find inhabitants who reveal, in an extreme form, unfortunate characteristics that Saro-Wiwa found in his fellow Nigerians. For example, one settlement is richly endowed with natural resources but those who live there will do nothing for themselves – they are dependent on outsiders to pluck the fruit that grows in abundance. Another island is divided between different religious groups, who destroy, out of sectarian rivalry, all that they have created. The (Thin) local inhabitants of a third island are controlled by the laughter of (Fat) incomers who force them to carry them wherever they want to go. Through these and other images, and through the cringing accounts journalists give of conditions in their own land (Nigeria), Saro-Wiwa launched a satirical onslaught worthy of Jonathan Swift on the complacency, stupidity, greed, destructiveness, ignorance, and other vices he detected among his fellow countrymen and women.

In looking at the voyage by canoe, Saro-Wiwa can be tied down to a specific point of view, but it would be inappropriate to do this in relation to every passage. The satire is sometimes loosely structured, tacked to an *ad hoc* framework; there are shifts in attitudes to characters and a general avoidance of the strictly allegorical. Among the un-ambiguously identifiable portraits is one of Margaret Thatcher who is present in a diaphanous disguise as 'Jane Billows'. However, we should not expect other characters to be portraits in the same way or assume that they will remain static, any more than Professor or Pita Dumbrok did in *Jebs*. Pita, significantly, continues to grow, emerging as an articulate visionary, a leader of thought capable of expressing deep truths and of providing a transforming challenge.

The value that comes through most strongly in the book as a whole is linked with Pita's transformation, the implication being that writers who state important truths can influence others for the better. The point is made most clearly by young Biney, who acknowledges that he has worked his way to a social vision through, in his words, 'Reading Pita Dumbrok. Thinking Pita Dumbrok. Analysing Pita Dumbrok.' (*Prison*, p. 143) Biney, like Martin Luther King, has a dream. He tells Azini:

I dream of a job for all young people; I dream of a good education for our people; I dream of a higher standard of living, I dream of peace, I dream of progress. I dream of a world where caring will be living, of a world where we will all hold hands and share, a world which will banish wars and hunger and disease. And I dream of you and me, our friends, our people, taking part in this world, not as spectators, not as objects of pity and commiseration, not as objects of laughter and scorn but as valued participants, contributing to the best of our ability and winning recognition for doing so. (*Prison*, p. 142)

This vision encapsulates many of the virtues Saro-Wiwa wanted to cultivate. Were it realized then power-hungry politicians would quake, prison walls would crumble, and mind-forged manacles would crack.

*Pita Dumbrok's Prison* is an unusual and, at times, difficult book. Because it was published by a Port Harcourt-based company with a rudimentary distribution network, international access has been impeded and few of those looking at, for example, narrative strategies in contemporary African fiction have included references to its innovations. One can only hope that it has been on sale throughout Nigeria and that it has been read aloud over the radio there. It was addressed very specifically to Nigerians by an eloquent, imaginative and thoughtful patriot who was an adventurous and energetic author. With *Jebs*, it belongs to a period of dialogue between Saro-Wiwa and his compatriots, impressive in its courage and anticipating a time when the dialogue would break down.

The next book sheds light on a different aspect of Saro-Wiwa's creativity. But before looking at the narrative, I want to pause and note that *Lemona's Tale* was published by Penguin. It is tempting to suggest that the publisher's interest was sharpened by the renown Saro-Wiwa achieved in death, by the perception of him as an eco-warrior martyred by a brutal regime in cahoots with a despicable, transnational oil company. The editor may have been intrigued by the possibility that certain elements in the book dimly reflected elements in Saro-Wiwa's life.

Lemona, whose tale is recorded by Ola, a young foreign-educated Nigerian woman, is sent to prison, released and then set up so that she is executed for a murder she has not committed! So far, with the change of name and gender, so Wiwa-esque. That Lemona is an Ogoni from the Khana-speaking area of the Niger Delta and that she is executed in Port Harcourt Prison provide further points at which the coincidence might seem to be prophetic or explicit. The parallels explain, I suspect, the publication of the book by a major publishing house, one that had already shown an interest in Saro-Wiwa's autobiographical writing. However, *Lemona's Tale* itself, although intriguing and demonstrating Saro-Wiwa's versatility and some of his energy, lacks the level of craftsmanship that characterizes his best work.

The central character, Lemona, is compelled by poverty to leave school early. An innocent abroad in Nigeria during the forties, she moves through domestic service, or slavery, to the 'protection' of a Port Harcourt hairdresser. She then spends a period with a contractor who offers her beautiful face and 'bra-bursting' figure for the sexual gratification of those to whom favours are owed. From there, it is a short step to becoming the mistress of Donatus Adoga, a high-flying executive with the United Africa Company. Adoga sets Lemona up with an apartment and an allowance, but, after three years, he becomes violently jealous of the attention being paid to her by one of her 'homeboys', Edoo Kabari. Adoga proves as brutal and vindictive when crossed as he had once been loving and generous – Kabari is killed and Lemona is reduced to penury. At this point an expatriate oil engineer, rather unimaginatively called John Smith, plays a part in Lemona's saga – he rescues her, provides for her, makes her 'feel like a woman', teaches her to play tennis, gives her English lessons, and then jilts her in favour of a woman met on leave. The distraught Lemona throws a knife at John Smith, he falls and is killed. Brought before a judge in what is still pre-independence Nigeria, Lemona is found guilty and spends the next twenty years in Port Harcourt Prison. She is then released, plays out the final scenes of her dramatic life, and, on the night before her execution, tells her story to Ola.

Since hers is a tale in which the long arm of coincidence intervenes at several points, and in which imprisonment does not prevent a 'bra-bursting' woman being pursued by men, there is more to the story. But this is as far as it is fair to go, only the novelist has the right to reveal the other twists and turns in the tale. None of them, incidentally, make the links between Lemona and Saro-Wiwa, pointed out above, any stronger.

In Lemona, Saro-Wiwa created a protagonist in a familiar mould: a deprived young woman who has the very worst start in life and who is then repeatedly exploited by a world in which compassion and concern are only briefly glimpsed. Somewhat strangely for fictional heroines in a genre dominated by Moll Flanders, Lemona is a woman who makes few decisions, and who rarely feels in control of people or events. At one point she actually says 'I did not happen to anything or to anyone. Each time I tried to happen, disaster resulted.' (p. 110) She is propelled into adventures by her beauty and the machinations of others rather than by the exercise of her will.

In certain respects the text represents a departure for Saro-Wiwa. Veteran author of several series of *Basi and Company*, chronicler of the lives of Nigeria's racketeers, swindlers and fraudsters, he frequently placed tricksters and conmen at the centre of his plots. On this occasion, however, he gave the organizers minor parts while focusing his attention on one of those they manipulated. His own background – particularly his upbringing, his experience in state administration and his career as a private businessman equipped him to write certain parts of *Lemona's Tale*. He was, for example, very familiar with Port Harcourt, the city in which his ravishingly beautiful protagonist has to sink or swim. However, it would appear that – although he rewrote the book while in prison, his own incarceration came too late to influence the passages in which he, hastily, sketchily, describes Lemona's time behind bars.

Although Saro-Wiwa writes easily and although his sentences often flow delightfully, this is not such an asset as usual since the bulk of this novel is supposed to be told in the words of a woman of limited education. The convention established is that Ola simply remembers what Lemona has told her and writes it down. This is supposed to be total recall at two levels, and the challenge is to suggest the voice of a Delta-born primary school-leaver as filtered through the memory of a highly educated young woman. In the event, Saro-Wiwa shows little interest in the various dimensions suggested by this 'layering'. He is satisfied with telling a surprising, shocking, dramatic story with all the resources of vocabulary and structure at his command. The decision to introduce Ola, who provides a frame for the tale and who plays a part within the story as a whole, offers opportunities that are rarely taken up. Only occasionally are we aware of her mediating presence or of her emotional involvement in the events she is told about and has to repeat.

I suspect that the script was published without careful revision and that this explains the misleading signals sent by certain usages. For example, in employing the word 'gist' as a verb to mean 'to make small talk', Lemona reflects Nigerian university student 'slang' of the nineteen fifties and sixties, while, at other times – as in the line 'it was to that life I bent my mind and my footsteps' (p. 33), the language conveys the flavour of eighteenth-century England. Elsewhere one is simply astonished by the vocabulary of a woman who, whatever life and lovers might subsequently have taught her, had little formal education. Unusual words used include 'coterie' (p. 51), 'iridescent' (p. 108), 'cynosure' (p. 125) and 'anon' (p. 126). All in all the text is, simply, the work of a consummate student of English usage, and there are minimal indications that the language has been filtered and selected. Often whole paragraphs flow past without, apparently, being marked by Lemona's experiences and, indeed, there is little that suggests Saro-Wiwa entered deeply and imaginatively into the life of the character for whom he found an author.

The twist that comes towards the conclusion, after Lemona has been released is, deliberately, deeply shocking. Near the end she realizes that she has been used by a disappointed man and that all has fallen out neatly for a Machiavellian revenger. As suggested above, it is possible that Saro-Wiwa was, like Lemona, forced to be part of a 'judicial charade', his tormentors were similarly Machiavellian.

The fourth and final book I want to look at is framed by Saro-Wiwa's arrest and release in June–July 1993. Completed nearly a year later, just days before the murder of the four Ogoni leaders for which Saro-Wiwa was tried, found guilty and executed, the 'Diary' is part history, and part prison log. It is also an account of a personal odyssey to discover international organizations willing to support a green campaigner and a human rights activist in his struggle against the twin monsters of domestic despotism and a multinational oil company.

The odd combination is sometimes confusing, sometimes contradictory, both engaging and engaged. Although widely presented in the English press – and in William Boyd's Introduction to *A Month and a Day*, as a 'writer', Saro-Wiwa used his eloquence and command of English so transparently for a purpose that he often operated as a propagandist. There is, for example, a good deal of 'special pleading' in the prison diary. Some statements look suspiciously like half truths and the impression lingers that for a description of the full complexity of the situation we will have to wait for someone else to put pen to paper.

Certainly, the volume is a pretty rough text and, since it contains battalions of hostages to fortune, is a gift to Saro-Wiwa's detractors. The author is, for example, badly served by Penguin's sub-editors who have allowed the figure of 51,000 Ogonis to be published on page 223. This is surely a misprint for 510,000 and it is a matter of some importance since it relates to the number of Ogonis who became environmentally active – 'almost the entire 51,000.'

Somewhat surprisingly for a movement that implies it was radical and democratic, decisions in the Ogoni organization of which Saro-Wiwa wrote were frequently taken by acclamation, and the ballot box was boycotted more often that it was honoured. There are those who argue that Saro-Wiwa claimed to speak for all Ogonis while, in truth, he articulated the desires of a tenth of the total population – a mere 51,000 out of the figure of 510,000 or so that is sometimes offered as a rough estimate of the population. For such critics, Penguin's decimation deviated into truth.

Saro-Wiwa presented himself as the Voice of his People, all 510,000 of them. Certainly he was the Publicity Secretary and later the President of a somewhat vaguely defined group, the Movement for the Survival of the Ogoni People (MOSOP). But, the ease with which the Publicity Secretary of MOSOP 'rewrote' his title and became the 'Spokesman for the Ogoni' is deeply disturbing. Saro-Wiwa did not always help his case by the way in which he presented it and readers are likely to spend some time comparing (and contrasting) statements made in different parts of the book. For example, to a Working Group on Indigenous Populations in Geneva, he delivered a description of his native land that included the following:

> the Ogoni people continue to live in pristine conditions in the absence of electricity, pipe-borne water, hospitals, housing and schools. The Ogoni are being consigned to slavery and extinction. (pp. 96–7)

Since there are references elsewhere in the book to the schools that Saro-Wiwa and others attended in Ogoniland, and to the hospital where his brother worked, there are parts of this statement that are quite clearly inaccurate. Undoubtedly there should be better educational and medical provision in the Delta, but the case cannot be argued by misrepresenting the situation. (He would also have done well to avoid the word 'pristine' since he clearly wanted to evoke only some of its associations.)

Once a single loose thread has been pulled clear from the fabric of his argument, one wonders how much of the text will unravel. The question is: Where does the 'economy with the truth' stop? In relation to the lines just quoted, one asks: Are there no houses? (Or is 'housing' used in a special sense?) Is there really slavery? (No payment of wages, no right to leave employment?) Are the Ogoni actually being wiped out? (Or are they, as others claim, increasing in numbers?) What exactly does he mean by 'pristine'? The answer is that Saro-Wiwa's *cri de coeur* is inextricably mingled with his cry of 'Wolf!'

Much as one admired Saro-Wiwa's courage and determination, his gifts as a creative writer and his achievements in business and television, the posthumous publication raises doubts about his conduct. For example, explaining the motives which prompted him to go into business during the late seventies, he wrote:

> I wasn't looking for a lot of money: just enough to ensure that my children could go to school without pain if I were to dedicate myself to the interests of the Ogoni people, and that I had a roof over my head so that no one could throw me and my family into the rain. (p. 56)

These feelings are commendable and are shared by many, indeed they motivate millions to 'struggle to gain'. However, the statement does not prepare the reader for estimating the sort of money, Saro-Wiwa was 'looking for'. This was revealed very clearly by the school he chose for his younger son – Eton. As it happens, the boy, Tedum, tragically died at the age of fourteen – a bereavement that Saro-Wiwa clearly felt profoundly. I mention the death only because, in writing about the support he received at the time of his loss, Saro-Wiwa refers to help from members of staff at Eton, and from teachers at Cheam and Roedean. The other schools, presumably also involved in the education of his children, suggest that Saro-Wiwa's ideas of a school and the kind of ('just enough') resources necessary to pay school fees were quite different from those of all but a minute fraction of Nigerian parents. When most West African parents talk of school fees they are thinking of having to make sacrifices to meet costs of education at local institutions. They are not thinking of having to write out cheques to the British private schools favoured by the Royal Family, cheques that quickly add up to tens of thousands of pounds.

Saro-Wiwa's book clearly repays close and critical reading. It is fascinating, for example, to observe the author's changing attitude to political structures, most strikingly his narrowing loyalties. During the Civil War, he supported the Federal Government and, at only twenty-six, was given a burdensome federal responsibility. After the war, he held ministerial-level posts in the relatively recently formed Rivers State, and later supported the campaign for a Port Harcourt State. With a certain inevitability, he subsequently advocated the creation of an Ogoni State. This follows a pattern, but if he was concerned about local government how did he justify his tenure of a post (referred to by Cameron Duodu and Janet Anderson in the British press) in a government-owned newsprint manufacturing operation? How did he reconcile his increasing dedication to Ogoni rights with becoming an Executive Director of the Directorate of Social Mobilisation? I think we should have been told.

The 'Diary' muddies the deep water that Saro-Wiwa found himself in on the 'national issue'. It should not be forgotten that, in simple terms, the volume is an account of the detention of the Publicity Secretary of MOSOP during 1993 on charges described in the following terms:

I heard it said that we had assembled at an Ogoni village which I had not visited all my life, there to plan I know not what. That we had designed a flag and written an anthem, and planned I know not what against the government of Nigeria or some place like that. All this amounted to a six-count charge of sedition and unlawful assembly. (p. 219)

So far, it would seem, so unreasonable, indeed so ridiculous. The dismissive tone suggests the charges originated in a paranoid imagination located somewhere in the heart of the federal territory of Abuja. But just how are we to take this arrogant pushing to one side of 'Nigeria or some place like that' and of the charges? How, in particular are we meant to read them when we recall that Saro-Wiwa had referred to Tombari Leton designing a MOSOP flag (p. 205), and when we remember that he had described his own composition ('Bari a dem Ogono') as 'the single anthem for Ogoni' (p. 206)? Saro-Wiwa appears to confess to some of the charges just pages before brushing aside the accusations listed above as unworthy of serious consideration.

As a result of following the author's political development and noting certain contradictions, one is prompted to ask: 'What exactly did this determined leader stand for? And, what precisely was his contribution to the national debate?' His answers might have been summed up with the sort of flourish beloved of a discredited generation of Nigerian politicians in the word 'ERECTISM'. The partial acronym stands for 'Ethnic Autonomy, Resource and Environmental Control.' Amplifying the concept, Saro-Wiwa wrote: 'We in Ogoni are reconstructing our society even as we fight the grim war of genocide'. (p. 149) He also talked about rehabilitating and reconstructing 'our proud heritage – the Ogoni nation', of re-emphasizing the practice of self-reliance, and of ensuring the study of the Eleme, Gokana and Khana languages. (pp. 149–150) All very admirable, but, even in the process of advocating the ideals, the whole issue of nationhood – represented by the E of ERECTISM, is called into question. If there are three languages in Ogoniland can there be a single nation? This is the sting in the tail of ERECTISM: an acknowledgement of linguistic diversity that raises a fundamental question about nationhood – one Saro-Wiwa does not address. The other issue that he fails to confront is hiding in the A that slips (unnoticed?) out of ERECTISM, the A for Autonomy. What did Saro-Wiwa mean by 'autonomy' in the context of the Nigerian Federation? Did it, for example, involve the dreaded 'S' word: 'Secession'?

There is evidence to suggest that Saro-Wiwa was perceived as a potential secessionist, indeed the federal attitude to him only makes sense if that is acknowledged. In his prison diary (and on other platforms), he sometimes avoided denying secessionist ambitions – and so encouraged people to believe he harboured them. On this issue much more will be said, and I will listen attentively!

Over a year after the typescript of *A Month* had been prepared, Saro-Wiwa appeared before the Tribunal at Port Harcourt and was eventually sentenced to death. The single most important factor in guaranteeing the impact of his sacrifice was the timing. The delivery of the Tribunal's verdict on the eve of the Commonwealth Heads of Government meeting in Auckland, and Sani Abacha's decision to have the Ogoni Nine executed while the meeting was in progress inevitably provoked a strong, united reaction. Had Abacha not thrown his horrid deed in every eye, a compromise would quite possibly have been worked out. As it was, the executioners took their blundering way to the scaffold and Nigeria was suspended from the Commonwealth.

After Saro-Wiwa's death – and to a lesser extent the deaths of those who died with him – there were moves to isolate Nigeria and to embarrass Shell. While it did not bring the Abacha regime to its knees or transform Shell's environmental accounting procedures, Saro-Wiwa's impact 'as a committed writer with some financial independence', was certainly significant. As *A Month and a Day* reveals through its eloquence and contradictions, he was an immensely gifted and very complex man, in whom charm, flair, determination and energy were combined. He contributed much before his life was cut short by a dictatorial and brutal regime, and his 'story', suitably modified for popular consumption, will inspire generations of Nigerians. His ghost will haunt Abuja.

Meanwhile the imprisonment described in *A Month and a Day* stands as an aborted prelude, a truncated dress rehearsal, revealing the anxiety of the Nigerian regime to eliminate Saro-Wiwa. They realized that they had to divide the Ogonis if they were to carry the day in the Delta, and the plan that eventually fell into place did indeed drive a wedge between the different inhabitants of Ogoniland. The injustice of the execution of the Ogoni Nine was transparent, but the federal conspiracy, fuelled by advertisements in the press, managed to divert and distract. The military regime has been able to divide and rule.

The memory of Ken Saro-Wiwa is constantly under attack from reactionary forces in his 'fantastically fantastic' homeland and those concerned must repeatedly refer to the texts he wrote, recognizing that they contain part of the truth about his character, genius and mission. Some of these texts began life as newspaper columns, ephemeral but widely read, they were 'rescued' and published by Saros International. Now, through the distribution network of the African Books Collective, they are widely available, and, together with *Lemona's Tale*, the prison diary, the trial and the execution at Port Harcourt, provide essential information. Apparently, the prison authorities, fearing that it would become a talisman to those seeking to keep Saro-Wiwa's great spirit alive, refused to hand over to his relatives the 'trade-mark' pipe Ken Saro-Wiwa smoked and chewed on. So long as his books remain, his spirit will intrigue and inspire.

James Gibbs
University of the West of England

Ulysses Chuka II. *For the Fairest*. Kampala: Fountain Publishers
and Aquarius Bookcase, 1991, 305 pp.
Lilian M. Tindyebwa. *Recipe for Disaster*. Kampala: Fountain
Publishers, 1994, 144 pp.
Timothy Wangusa. *A Pattern of Dust*. Kampala: Fountain
Publishers, 1994, 87 pp., with notes & index.
Goretti Kyomuhendo. *The First Daughter*. Kampala: Fountain
Publishers, 1996, 136 pp.
All titles distributed by African Books Collective Ltd, The Jam Factory,
27 Park End Street, Oxford, OX1 1HU, UK.

A batch of books from Uganda is an excitement. Little creative writing
has reached the outside world in recent years. The four works reviewed
here were published in 1991, 1994, and 1996. There are two novels by
women writers, one thriller and a collection of poems, all published by
Fountain Publishers in Kampala, a press which is doing a great deal to
encourage writers. The firm must be commended, for it is important that
such work is available in Uganda at a reasonable price, although the
standard of editing and proof reading could be improved. (In *The First
Daughter* the reader turned from page 64 to 91 and then two pages 67/68
which is confusing.)
    Only one of the four unrelated works could be claimed to be of much
literary value, but the two novels about a couple of unhappy young
women, *Recipe for Disaster*, by Lilian Tindyebwa, and *The First
Daughter*, by Goretti Kyomuhendo, could be used as a basis of a
discussion on the position of women, although any self-respecting girl
would easily spot their foolishness. *For the Fairest* can be described as
fast moving exciting entertainment of the Raymond Chandler variety.
    If one took the picture of life presented in these works as authentic it
would be a pretty bleak picture: corruption everywhere, violence not far
below the surface in town and country, and promiscuous sex. The
ignorance of the rural communities parallels the sexual looseness of the
town. Does no one at home or at school do anything about sex education? Any parent reading *Recipe for Disaster* or *The First Daughter*
would be put off sending a daughter to a boarding school, in view of the
lack of supervision which enables cruel bullying and does not notice
the absence of girls for a whole weekend.
    Gold smuggling, violence and indiscriminate hetero- and homosexual
relations are everywhere in *For the Fairest* by Ulysses Chuka. In his
created world guns, ammunition and women seem equally obtainable,
especially in the Sodom of Nairobi, and violence flares up regularly. But
these are fictitious worlds. The novels telling the stories of two silly
girls are not designed as escapism. They have moments of verisimi-
litude. The opening scene gathering grasshoppers in *The First Daughter*
for instance or the dormitory bullying when Kase gets to Duhaga; the
relationship between the pregnant girl and Grandmother Mukaaka is
effectively drawn and the scene in which Kase returns to the village to

find desolation – these ring true. It is the same in *Recipe for Disaster*. The surreal dreams of both Jenny and Hellen are vivid, although the mother's dream is not strictly relevant. The search for a new school after Hellen has been expelled for smoking is believable. This is a materialistic world with little depth of character or feeling. Does it reflect the taste of the public for which these works are written: melodrama with sex, guns, fast cars and continual violence; or stark tragedy with a moral lesson rather too simplistically presented to be effective – the dying scene in *Recipe for Disaster* really is over the top. The misunderstandings which produce the problems and later their solutions in *The First Daughter* are rather obviously manipulated. But each novel has its merits. *For the Fairest* is fast moving, has a racy and sophisticated style and is told from the viewpoint of Alfa once the prologue is over. It is verbose, the scenes in Ino's home out-Bond James Bond, but there is undoubted narrative power. This writer is not called Ulysses for nothing, even if one questions where an ex-policeman turned smuggler learned his classics. One may criticize the rather clumsy device of confession to complete the denouement but by then the story has moved into fantasy as Alfa leaps from a pursuing car through the open door of a plane in which his sister-in-law Zizi is flying off with his diamonds. She meets him with a gun but he is saved by Ino still in the car below who is able to see all this and shoot Zizi, who confesses all as the plane taxis to a stop. But, at least, all the ends *are* tied off.

The viewpoint of the other two novels is less well handled. In *Recipe* it shifts from parents to daughter, from daughter to boyfriend, and it might have been more effective if all the events had been seen through Hellen's eyes. Kevin is an interesting portrayal. He is quite open about his polygamy, would have negotiated fairly with Hellen's parents, but we are expected to sympathize with Hellen and because we see things through his eyes he generates sympathy when he leaves his dying first wife to discover that the child just born to his third is a half-caste. The cuts, and the necessary following flashbacks, do not add anything to the structure. Characterization is uncertain and from the moment Hellen runs away from Kevin's wrath, is befriended by the hospital askari and found by her parents, one has ceased to take the story seriously. Sometimes writers claim that what they are relating is based on actuality, but it is insufficient to claim it really happened; it must ring true. The end of this tale does not.

The portrait of the father in *The First Daughter* begins convincingly enough but when Kase returns pregnant the man who has been presented earlier as a tender lover and husband and a proud father now becomes an unforgiving tyrant. The coincidences that manipulate Kasemiire's trials are hard to accept. Would Steven be so importunate when both know how vital the exams are? Or so weak in his reaction to her pregnancy? If the Mutyaba parents are sufficiently caring to send away their son because he is obsessed with Kase, can we really believe in the appearance of the naked Mr Mutyaba at her bedroom door? But there are some vivid moments: Kase's relations with both her mother and grandmother are well handled, and there is some depth in the characterization of the village women. But there are too many co-incidences and the happy ending is somewhat hastily scraped together. Characters no longer needed are dropped or killed off.

Stylistically both women writers are satisfied with a loose use of platitude and cliché, and could pay much more attention to the actual meaning of what they are saying. Steven tells Kase he has never known her to cry even though the author has made her cry almost continually and *he* goes on to say 'I never want you to cry again in your life. You did enough of it in the last eight years.'

All three prose writers could learn from Wangusa's delicately precise use of words. His collection of poems, *A Pattern of Dust*, contains poems he has written over 25 years, and is wide-ranging. Again however the publishers must be criticized for poor proof reading. (For instance 'your shall' instead of 'you', page 6; but 'you legs' on page 12; the kings are 'accentric' on page 25; and there are inconsistencies in spacing and lay out which could have been corrected. Cover designers could be acknowledged, as the most recent and most effective cover of *The First Daughter* has been.

The poems are divided into six sections. The first, 'Nativity Soil', contains poems concerned with Professor Wangusa's home area of Masaba. The rhythms of some of these poems remind the reader of W. B. Yeats and Christopher Okigbo, but the imagery is from the mountain, and its village communities, with their beliefs and ethics. The next section is entitled 'Sovereign Flags', the content of which might indicate why the poet has never been completely happy in the political world. He sees the absurdities. There is humour and satire here, and many of his friends have found his version of 'Psalm 23' memorable. The opening 'Song to Mukoteni', the home-made wheelbarrow, carries witty satire in its hyperbole; Wangusa entertains in the claim that millet beer has conquered 'the foottrodden banana'. There is a new originality of voice although it is sometimes marred by overuse of syntactic repetition. But 'Bill Shakespeare's smug iambic pentameter' and the picture of the 'blacksmith in a white-washed mask/dancing round a cauldron' are memorable phrases and there is a controlled lyricism which is multilevelled. Section 3, 'Flesh and Metal', is notable for the subtlety under the apparent simplicity, as in the end of 'A Taxi-Driver on his Death', where human blood is under the metal, or the satirical picture concluding The Third World War. The humour and bitterness behind the poems on space travel and flying are lacking in the shock of 'Kilembe Mines'. The section ends with the lyrical voice of 'He Longs to Return to Butiru', which is not nostalgia but an awareness of the strength of his roots. 'Female Kind' is the title of the next section and the poems range from a tribute to Mrs Cook after a visit to Southwick, those written for Women's Day, and the lovely nature imagery of the final poem. Okara wrote about snow from an African view; Wangusa evokes the whole of Africa as he looks at Wisconsin. 'The Masqueraders', Section 5, contains humorous verses: a fine piece of satire in 'Bishop of Cows', and the amusing image play of 'At the Kwaheri Bar'.

This collection maps the poet's reactions to experiences all over the world. The Makerere Travelling Theatre took him to many parts of East Africa and the resulting poems which mark his response have depth. 'Nyenga' records a visit to the Leprosarium. 'The Rain Came' records in verse a particularly effective mime to a story by Grace Ogot, in Kisumu. The mining settlement of Kilembe had already given rise to one poem but 'Kilembe' in this section asks which is more real, the alien miners or the people who go on as they always have? The Pirandello image with which it opens is one of the well-employed literary references Wangusa uses discreetly, in this instance to express the doubt such a place arouses 'as the border dissolves/Between dream and reality'. The last poem looks on Margarita and expresses that yearning that all mountains generate and perhaps Ruwenzori more than many. The final section 'Intimations' contains further expression of joy in natural beauty and the sincere questioning of 'the eternity/ of the backward glance'. In the brilliant sequence 'Unto the Utmost Parts' with its biblical echoes is mapped the progress of Christianity in Uganda from the satire of 'the stranger with the scalded skin' who came in the year of *Das Kapital* to the triumph of 'Post Mortem'. 'Time and Distance' takes us from Earth where experience leads to the dream 'space shall have no dominion' and Heaven where the vision, like that in *Ash Wednesday*, is expressed in apparently simple images which take the reader beyond the dance 'through the rainbow arch'. The last poem 'Hell', where the poet sees himself 'slowly crunched by granite jaws', is more simplistic than the view of Heaven. This section began with the poem which gave the title to the collection and which expresses a joy in accidental beauty that is universal: the pattern of dust cast by sun through broken glass.

Timothy Wangusa's poetry has the double merit of being accessible to the literate reader but revealing more and more as that reader studies it. While it arises out of personal experience many other people will recognize they share his feelings. All life is his territory. There is to be another volume of political verse, we are told. We shall look forward to hearing again this individual voice that is witty and lyrical, sophisticated and Ugandan.

Margaret Macpherson
Windermere, UK

---

Ayi Kwei Armah. *Osiris Rising*. Popenguine: Per Ankh, 1995.

*Osiris Rising* is yet another novel by Armah with a declared and palpable design on the reader. Like *Two Thousand Seasons* and *The Healers* before it, this is a moral fable, simplified and stark, in which the forces of destruction are ranged against the representatives of wholeness. Like its predecessors, this is a pan-African story, but in a more emphatic sense. Armah has said that he has always been aware of himself as not simply Fante or Akan or Ghanaian, but as African: this novel is perhaps his most explicit attempt at creating a truly panoramic pan-African canvas that stretches back in time to include ancient Egypt or Kemt, and spreads across the diaspora to include African-American attitudes and aspirations. The main action, however, takes place in the neo-colonial Africa of today where in May–June 1997 we witnessed a real-life allegory of murderers and angels as Mobutu faced Kabila before a chorus of minders that included a representative of the United States government, a representative of the United Nations, and President Mandela, as perhaps the only truly haloed character. Some readers have objected to the simplicity of design which Armah has employed in his recent writing; but like the driver of a caravan with his eye on his destination and no ear for chattering bystanders, Armah writes on, intending perhaps to redefine his audience. Nevertheless, there is a question that haunts the reader of this novel: Is there anything truly new in it?

*Osiris Rising* is the story of three characters representative of three important tendencies in the modern African situation as Armah sees it. Of the three, the narrative focus first falls on Ast, an African-American woman, historian by training, who gives up America's opulence built upon racism and violent competitiveness and returns to the land of her ancestors. It is significant that Ast is a historian for in her view, as in Armah's, Africa's recovery from her present prostration before the West requires first and foremost the retrieval and re-adoption of her ancestral identity and values. This, it will be recalled, was also the message of *Two Thousand Seasons*, but as bearer of a restorative message Ast is also one of 'the healers' and therefore links *Osiris Rising* with *The Healers*.

She is, however, no neo-colonial missionary come to save a helpless Africa, though there is such an African–American character in the novel. Her symbiotic partner in the novel is the African, Asar, another of the three main characters. Asar, the male counterpart to Ast, is an exemplary figure who is very reminiscent of Densu in *The Healers* and has a genealogy in the world of Armah's writings that goes all the way back to the nameless hero of *The Beautyful Ones are not yet Born*. Ast and Asar are only part of a community of healers or 'beautyful' ones, a progressive group of thinkers dedicated to rescuing Africa from tyrannical rulers who are themselves mere agents of Western economic interests. These intellectuals, in consonance with Armah's pan-Africanist intent, are drawn from different parts of the African continent and bear names like Bantu Rolong, Lamine Djatta, Iva Mensa, Dineo Letsie and Imo Moko. Armah's emphasis here, as in other books, is on Africa as one community which he sees as essentially (and anachronistically) black.

Ranged against these thinkers or healers are, of course, the destroyers, 'The slave-foremen' and 'crumb-hungry' Africans, ever ready for the sake of personal profit to enslave or destroy fellow Africans. Like the healers, the destroyers are of ancient and long-standing stock in the universe of Armah's fiction: Kamuzu in *Two Thousand Seasons* is an earlier incarnation as is Ababio in *The Healers*, but Koomson in *The Beautyful Ones* is the founding father. In *Osiris Rising* the forces of destruction are led by the third major character of the novel called Seth Spencer Soja, head of security in the corrupt, typically neo-colonial state in which the action of the novel takes place. Each one of Seth's string of alliterative names says something of his character: 'Spencer' reveals the neo-colonial attachment to England, and 'Soja' is soldier, indicative of his belief in force rather than reason. (Of his first name, more later). Addicted to the good life, Seth is really a parasite on the state who hides his limited ability behind the show of power and wealth. He is above all committed to the destruction of Asar, his opposite and an old schoolmate; but, more generally, his mission is to preserve the present neo-colonial state of his country and make it safe for the greater profit of the multinationals – as well as the lesser benefit of the African elite who think they rule.

In this novel, the forces of destruction also assume pan-African dimensions. Ras Jomo Cinque Equiano – whose long name indicates a composite of treacherous tendencies – is an African–American character descended from African slave dealers. He has returned to Africa bringing a hideous concoction of beliefs and practices which he claims to be authentically African and which he wishes to restore to Africa. In reality, what he seeks is a short-cut to personal fame and status through collaboration with the present dictatorship. He stands at the opposite pole to Ast, the other African–American, who wishes to contribute to Africa's recovery by immersing herself in community work.

*Osiris Rising* may present an opposition that is already familiar to Armah's readers, but the use of ancient Egyptian mythology is an obvious innovation. Asar, the central character, bears a name which sounds Akan; Armah in fact plays on this resemblance when the character is called 'Wofa Esar', or Uncle Esar, by some children (p. 248). Asar (or Ausar) is, however, the name of the god of fertility and giver of civilization, later the supreme god and ruler of the dead who later came to be known as Osiris when Kemt (or ancient Egypt) came under Hellenic dominance. Again Ast is properly the name of the goddess who became known as Isis, queen of the gods and great mother figure, and wife of Asar. Seth is Set, brother and murderer of Asar. The chapter headings are in ancient Egyptian, each chapter connecting contemporary reality with Egyptian mythology. Thus for instance the crucial chapter in which the African historian, Tete (Akan for 'ancient'?), underlines the importance of linking with the past is entitled 'Jehwty' which is the name of the moon goddess, the inventor of writing and protector of Ast during her pregnancy. Armah's novel ends with the death of Asar at a time when Ast is pregnant. According to the myth, she will give birth to Hrw or Hor (to be known later as Horus) who will oppose and eventually triumph over Set.

The use of myth to give form and meaning to contemporary experience is not new in African literature. Wole Soyinka uses Yoruba mythology in just this manner. The choice of this particular myth is an expression of Armah's belief in the necessity of reclaiming ancient

Egypt for black Africa and in the need for Africans to reconnect with their Egyptian heritage.

Like Armah's previous novels, then, *Osiris Rising* is yet another proposal for the defeat of Set, god of destruction. The neo-colonial situation which Seth Spencer Soja defends has its roots, according to Armah, in the ancient division of African societies into royalty and others – a division which the present ruling elite of Africa perpetuates by keeping the generality of their own people in poverty while they take short-cuts to power and wealth as local agents of multinational corporations. Seth Spencer Soja, typically, finds the neo-colonial status of Africa entirely satisfactory. The only thing that was wrong with colonialism itself, according to him, was that it denied people like him access to power. 'Independence' has eliminated that problem. *Osiris Rising* calls for the defeat of this selfish and divisive outlook which ultimately weakens Africa, and its replacement by the outlook represented by Asar, Ast and the society of progressive thinkers. This new attitude is of course not new, as any reader of *Two Thousand Seasons* knows: it emphasizes community and true equality and insists that talent is best used in service to society rather than for exclusive benefit or glory.

The egalitarianism at the heart of this attitude should inform human relations at all levels including the most personal, and particularly in relations between men and women. Armah illustrates this with the exemplary love relationship between Asar and Ast which he imbues with great tenderness and mutual respect, deliberately contrasting it with Seth Spencer Soja's attempted rape of Ast. Seth, who sees people only as objects to be used, can only relate to them at all levels through force and domination.

Asar, Ast and the community of healers also of course represent Armah's belief in the necessity for Africans to rediscover their past in a fundamental way as one means of throwing off the dominance of Europe and America. To emphasize this theme, two chapters of the novel, in blatant didacticism, are devoted to the efforts of the progressive intellectuals to design model syllabi for the study of the Humanities at African universities. And in these syllabi, as one would expect, emphasis is placed on Africa, particularly ancient Egypt, as well as on Asian, Amerindian and Pacific societies. Western culture and society, though not excluded, are accorded diminished importance.

Finally we return to the question as to whether *Osiris Rising* offers us anything that is really different from what we have already received from previous novels by the author. The fictional landscape is very familiar. For instance, the clock at the airport which does not work could well have been from *Fragments*. The pus which oozes sickeningly from Seth as he tries to rape Ast is the kind of physical detail used to express moral disease which we are familiar with from *The Beautyful Ones*. The message of the novel and the characters through which it is expressed are also familiar. So what is new? Certainly, the emphasis on a radically different content for African education is original, as is the use of the framework of Egyptian mythology as a stimulus to the reader to explore further. But perhaps what is most interesting in the context of Armah's writing is the synthesis of the contemporary with the mythical, the realistic with the allegorical. But perhaps another question arises? Is this novel not merely an exercise in wishful thinking? Hasn't Seth Spencer Soja already won the final victory? Aren't the multinationals, ably aided by local rulers, already in control all over the globe? If capitalism is the way forward then can divisions be avoided, and will Africans ever (to borrow an image from poet, Felix Mnthali) own the skyscrapers that spring up from to time in their capital cities? Will the majority of Africans ever leave the slums? The questions multiply as one's fears deepen when confronting the monolithic world landscape following the demise of the Eastern bloc. Perhaps Africa cannot expect now to gain total mastery over her resources. Perhaps the best we can hope for is to eliminate the slums. But even for that, Armah's novel is relevant. Even for that, selfless, community-oriented leadership is required. To improve the situation of Africa's peoples we need to wrest as much as we can from the grasp of the multinationals; and this means we must come to the bargaining table as a self-confident and unified pan-African community. Osiris must rise.

A. N. Mensah

Department of English, University of Botswana

Peter Slingsby. *The Joining.* Cape Town: Tafelberg, 1996.

A multiracial group of South African children on an ecological camping holiday step back in time to the distant past. Large game roams freely. The children fall in with a group of /Xam people, of whose probable lifestyle and culture an exposition is given. A leitmotif of descriptions, explanations and sitings of actual /Xam rock paintings runs through the book. The children have adventures featuring predatory animals, hostile tribes, mystical powers etc. before making a crucial decision.

The reader is strongly reminded that we are all members of one race, that harmony is the basic principle of community, and that we really ought to respect each other, since we are all so worthy of respect. A recipe, perhaps, for the new South Africa, prepared for the young in easy-to-swallow form?

Lying beneath the good intentions of the author are some unsatisfactory attitudes. The setting includes an undifferentiated mass of /Xam people: 'the rest of the clan', 'the men and women', 'the people', 'the band of strangers'. They are given no further definition. Are they people, landscape or background? In a novel that purports to be so respectful of indigenous culture, why should there be this confusion? But the characterization of even major figures is rudimentary, as though the author had worked out one or two qualities per person and then applied them mechanically. Inevitably dynamic interaction between the characters is lacking and they move from event to event with little sense of progress, development, or discovery. Perhaps their itinerary is determined less by the internal logic of character and plot working together than by the location in real space of those rock paintings the author wished to describe. This brings an odd stasis, dullness, to the novel which even the use of the magical device of omniscient dreaming cannot disperse; instead of extending or questioning the action it tends to repeat it. Jeremy, the central character, is a bit of a seer, and has prophetic dreams. But omniscience, like cheating at games or looking up the answers before finishing a puzzle, needs to be used judiciously or it becomes a bore.

Coupled with Jeremy's dreams are fainting fits and nosebleeds. The /Xam are unduly impressed by this behaviour, which brings us to the heart of what is wrong with the book.

> 'No one bows to Gau,' (Jeremy) complained. 'Why do they bow to me?' Xiko laughed. 'They say that you are like a chameleon,' he said. 'Not only are your eyes green like a chameleon's, but you can change the colour of your skin!'

Where have we seen this picture before, a green-eyed, white-skinned hero becoming a king in Africa by sheer intellectual, physical, moral and spiritual superiority? In a dozen works by authors such as Rider Haggard, John Buchan and, dare I say it, Edgar Rice Burroughs. Jeremy, initially tagged as having Black ancestry ('Rick obviously thought he was white. Rick didn't know that his aunt and his mother were nearly as dark as Christina.'), is overtly identified as white throughout the rest of the book: 'I think you have come from a far place, across the blue sea, although I do not yet know how you got here.' Neither is he supplied with anything like a Black context (unless this is coded into the street names), yet there are several indications of the strangeness, 'otherness', of Blackness in the text: 'Jeremy danced and saw Sitheli's eyes, the whites flashing in the firelight'; 'sat on the platform and cried until a large black lady . . . put him on a train that would take him home'.

So, on the one hand, *The Joining* is in the tradition of 'gateway' books, where a group of children step magically into a parallel world. The long pedigree includes T. H. White, C. S. Lewis, E. Nesbit, J. M. Barrie and ultimately Lewis Carroll. But the other half of its ancestry is the popular imperialist adventure – romances of the Allan Quatermain type.

Different authors have put the 'gateway' device to various uses: as a framework for the most fantastic adventures; to enable the child heroes to undergo trials which would be too dangerous and painful if set in the real world; as a means of applying lateral thinking to natural dilemmas; to give a highly entertaining history lesson; to explore a given proposition in allegorical terms. In *The Joining* the didactic motive is very evident: the story is a history lesson with a moral at the end. There is also an obvious reference to Golding's *Lord of the Flies*; We read:

> 'my name is Jeremy Samuel Paulson. I live at 5 Hampshire Road, Lansdowne. I live with my aunt while my mother is overseas. My telephone number is 762

... 762 ...' His mind reeled as he tried to remember the number ... and Jeremy faints again.

If this is a conscious borrowing, perhaps Slingsby is trying to signal the seriousness of his intentions. If it is not a conscious borrowing, then the editors should have reacted to it.

It is difficult to know how to recommend this book, which is intended for the 12 – 16 age group. Would a child dull enough to accept the hidden premise be reading a book about culture and rock paintings? Would a child thrilled by lion hunts and trials of manhood accept a hero who keeps fainting and getting bad sunburn? Of course it is possible, given the history of the past 500 years or so, to have a white character as a major player in an African narrative but it is carried out here with a degree of intellectual dishonesty. The fantasy of a Great White Chief at the heart of so-called Black experience is ultimately racist and, Sanlam Prize notwithstanding, brings this well-intentioned novel down to the level of an ecological Tarzan movie. As such it is unlikely to be acceptable to the majority of Black readers of any age.

Folake Shoga
Bristol, UK

---

Eckhard Breitinger, ed. *Defining New Idioms and Alternative Forms of Expression*. ASNEL Papers I. Amsterdam & Atlanta: Editions RODOPI, 1996. 293 pp.

Peter O. Stummer & Christopher Balme, eds. *Fusion of Cultures?* ASNEL Papers II. Amsterdam & Atlanta: Editions RODOPI, 1996, 344 pp.

Albert Gérard. *Afrique plurielle. Etudes de littérature comparée.* III. Amsterdam & Atlanta: Editions RODOPI, 1996, 199 pp.

*1. How Far are Bayreuth and Munich from 'Berlin'?*

Just a few hours' drive if you take the A9 highway but a long way away if you look at past colonial history and you measure the gap between this *fin de siècle* and 1884, when European imperial powers carved up the African continent in a Berlin conference room. It is in that spirit of revisiting Berlin, as it were, that the Bayreuth and Munich participants in the two conferences for the Association for the Study of New Literatures in English (ASNEL) reconsidered, at a one-year interval (1992 and 1993), the issues of syncretism, hybridity, cross-fertilization, creolization and the end-of-century fusion of cultures.

These two events yielded two heavy volumes that constitute Numbers 23 and 26 of Editions RODOPI's Cross/Cultures Series and stand as hearty tributes to German scholarship in the field of postcolonial studies. It is also in keeping with that spirit that the second volume starts with theoretical considerations about such time-honoured concepts from the social sciences as 'mapping out' and 'construction' and with an examination of Africa as the site of cultural fusion before the scramble. To wit, Detlev Gohrbandt's rediscovery of the little known iconographic and linguistic maps of the 'Dark Continent' created in R. M. Ballantyne's juvenile fiction of the 1850s and Tobias Döring's insightful re-evaluation of the semi-autobiographical novel from the 1930s, *Africa Answers Back* by Akiki Nyabongo. This Ugandan scholar does 'answer back to European discourse by reversing a missionary sucesss-story into the narrative of African empowerment and emancipation' (II, p. 141) and by so doing, Nyabongo shows that revanchism and striking back were already common strategies that postcolonial theory was to reinvent later.

I had a *déjà vu* experience when looking at Eckhard Breitinger's volume on *Defining New Idioms* because he had already published some of the Bayreuth Conference proceedings in *Theatre and Performance in Africa* (1994).[1] Despite the validating presence of 'diasporic subjects' from Africa, Asia and the Caribbean, one could lament the overwhelming presence of German scholars, so much so that at times the same contributors (e.g., Gohrbandt and Brückner) had their papers published in both volumes. On the other hand, the presence of East European scholars demonstrated the general but unspoken will to transcend 'Berlin'. Overall, the second volume on *Fusion of Cultures?* is more structured, more convivial with its frontispiece by Rufus Ogundele from the collection of Peter O. Stummer, who provided a stimulating Introduction but also enticing photographs of e.g., Witi Ihimaera, Bharati Mukherjee, Margaret Atwood and John Figueroa, the doyen of Caribbean letters, complete with white beard and walking stick.

The highly competent introductory essay by Christopher Balme on 'Inventive Syncretism', developed under the aegis of new anthropologists such as James Clifford in *The Predicament of Culture* (1988) and Clifford Geertz in *The Interpretation of Cultures* (1973), gives the volume both its tone and structure and has an ad hoc feel to it that the first volume lacks. Despite the overall coherence of this second volume, I can only see a very tenuous link between the conference theme and, for instance, Wolfgang Hochbruck's 'Armed Conflict and Cultural Encounters: Zimbabwean War Fiction' or Werner Sedlack's reading of prison memoirs by African political detainees such as Ngugi wa Thiong'o, Molefe Pheto and Wole Soyinka as a 'culture of resistance', after Barbara Harlow's phrase. The concept of syncretism as engendering 'hyphenated identities' is here stretched to its most 'inventive' extremes as it covers the notions of allusion and collage, as in 'Ngugi's selection of mottos and quotations ranging from Friedrich Engels, Karl Marx, ... to William Blake or Shakespeare and the Palestinian poet Mahmoud Darwish' (II, p. 185). This is arguably more representative of the broad range of Ngugi's readings than 'of this fusion of cultures for the purpose of critical social analysis and political resistance' (II, p. 185). Syncretism should never be shrunk to an artful collage or mosaic of quotes.

This short rubric on 'Autobiography and Cultural Plurality' would have gained in relevance if the authors had considered at greater depth how these collectivist memoirs rewrite Western autobiography. Indeed, since the 1970s this already highly individualistic genre has displayed an even greater preoccupation with the self, exemplified in the boom in various forms of therapy, the enormous increase in confessional writing[2] culminating with the 'tendenzwende' in Germany and the 'Me-Decade' in the United States. But outside the West and outside of male writing, the rage over English cultural imperialism has eventually made way for a 'cultural syncretism', as Gilmore would have it.[3] Women's autobiographics would have gone a long way in further balancing intercultural transfer.

## 2. The Pressures of Language: Yorubanglish, Kamtok and Ndenglish

After a boisterous opening by political activist Don Mattera, *Defining New Idioms* embarks on 'Rediscovering the Idiom of Orality'. By contrasting Achebe's 'additive method' with the 'inclusive English' (I, p. 59) of the younger Nigerian author Biyi Bandele Thomas in his first novel *The Man Who Came In From the Back of Beyond* (1991), Detlev Gohrbandt is merely pouring old terminological vintage into new bottles. As he himself acknowledges, his endeavour is 'an entirely unoriginal thesis' (I, p. 57) and he lamely concludes: 'How effective this new idiom will be, and how it can compare and compete with other kinds of rewritten English, are questions for future criticism' (I, p. 60). Little does he know that research in Africa, Europe and the United States has not only repeatedly tackled but belaboured these issues. No mention is made of Eileen Julien's *African Novels and the Question of Orality* (1992), my own *African Palimpsest: Indigenization of Language in the West African Europhone Novel* (1991) or Kenneth Harrow's *Thresholds of Change in African Literature* (1994), admittedly published after the event but before the proceedings saw the light of day. This habit of writing in a critical vacuum is a recurrent tick in both volumes and this is unforgivable in our post-Gutenberg galaxy, saturated as it is with informational overchoice.

David Tiomajou offers a diachronic view of language use in the Republic of Cameroon and wrestles with language planning. This is not an easy task, if one considers the 239 or so languages spoken in the Cameroon, including the two official languages (English and French) and Cameroonian Pidgin English (CPE). Tiomajou is pessimistic about the feasibility of the linguistic project, Propelca, whose ambitious purpose is to teach Cameroonian languages (e.g., Duala, Fefe, Lamnso and Ewondo) to young Cameroonians and he deems that such a task 'should be left to individual parents' (I, p. 253). But how can parents be expected to become pedagogues overnight, testing their children's skills in kitchens-turned-into-classrooms? He is also sceptical about the 'official bilingualism' concept which he stretches to include 'English and French and to some extent Spanish, German and Latin' (I, p. 257). I doubt very much Latin is a spoken language in Cameroon unless it is understood as Dan Quail did. (It may be recalled that, after a trip to Latin America, Quail regretted he had not studied Latin harder in school so that he could converse with 'those people'.) If I do not share Tiomajou's pessimism about the impossibility of developing the teaching of Cameroonian languages in formal education, I do share his elation about the use of CPE as a 'powerful lingua franca', 'without official recognition as yet' such as 'Camspeak' and 'Camtalk' (also kamtok). Also, I do sympathize with his plea to 'recognize CPE officially' although this pertinent step does not, in my opinion, exclude the development of the teaching of Cameroonian languages. One regret is that Tiomajou never mentions Loreto Todd's lifelong work devoted to Cameroonian Pidgin in, for example, *Modern Englishes: Pidgins and Creoles* (1984).

As the late pioneer of African historiography, Albert Gérard, reminds us once more in his *Afrique plurielle*, an inevitable creolization of European languages on African soil is bound to give the lie to 'the gloomy grammarians', to use W. H. Auden's phrase (III, p. 147). It is not by chance that Gérard, an internationally celebrated exponent of comparative literature, should crown this clever assortment of papers read and modified articles with a reflection on 'Tiers monde et littérature comparée' which denounces the hegemony of linguistic unity in defining national literatures (III, p. 191) and begs for tools better adapted to the new translinguistic and interdisciplinary dimension of comparative literature (III, p. 199).

Translinguistic methods entail the use of translation. In that regard, the contributions on translation in the first volume are disappointing. Vladimir Klima is supposed to provide a (Czech) translator's view on 'Nigerian Pidgin English' but never develops his views except to say in a concluding paragraph that while using standard Czech 'I have chosen colloquial forms, occasionally using socially coloured slang expression' (I, p. 273). No concrete examples are produced to grace a short and outmoded article that fails to show recent developments in EnPi as recorded by Nigerian linguists such as Augusta Omamor and also reduces literary production in EnPi to Onitsha market pamphleteering. Ezenwa-Ohaeto in poetry and Tunde Fatunde in drama would not be pleased to be left out and the avenging ghost of Ken Saro-Wiwa, the author of *Sozaboy: A Novel in Rotten English* (1985), must be haunting the Czech Republic's diplomatic service, of which Klima is a distinguished member. Some of Klima's statements are also simply untrue, as when he claims that 'Nigerian Pidgin English . . . has not been anyone's mother-tongue' (I, p. 272) when in fact some eight million native speakers of EnPi have been attested in the areas of Warrin, Sapele, and Port Harcourt.

As if to provide a strong counter-example to the dominance of English as a written medium on African soil, Mikhail Gromov traces the 'Swahilization' of Tanzanian life which has 'allowed' the English imported from Makerere University in neighbouring Uganda to become a viable alternative form of expression. The distribution was originally between ' "elitarian" literature in English . . . and popular literature (in Swahili) . . .', but the 1980s have witnessed 'the birth of Tanzanian popular literature in English' (I, p. 268). These healthy permutations inevitably beg the question of translation in Swahili literature, which is taken up by Andrei Zhuko who surveys, alongside written literature in the ninth-century Swahili script, translations from English to Swahili of religious texts from the mid-1840s; of European folklore and literature in the first half of the twentieth century through to the 1940s with free translations by the founder of modern Swahili literature, Robert Shaaban; up to the recent, post-colonial phenomenon of translating famous works by such writers as Chinua Achebe, Ngugi wa Thiong'o, Ayi Kwei Armah, Thomas Mofolo and even Gogol.

If Kamtok and EnPi point to a syncretic future in the linguistic arena and translation concretely ensures intercultural cross-over, the stage remains an ideal site for the criss-crossing of multiple linguistic instabilities. Out of the rich popular Yoruba Travelling 'total-theatre' of Duro Ladipo and Hubert Ogunde and the 'high-brow' texts of Wole Soyinka, Wale Ogunyemi, Femi Osofisan, Nigerian playwright Bode Sowande labels Ola Rotimi's epic tragedies in 'Yorubanglish' the most 'syncretised' of theatrical experiences (II, p. 23). It is a pity Sowande did not have access to Chris Dunton's well-informed chronicle of this vibrant and combative theatrical milieu *Make Man Talk True: Nigerian Drama in English Since 1970*. It was published in 1992, a year before the Munich Conference.

Flora Veit-Wild, for her part, indulges in the pleasures of anachronism by lifting the title of her paper 'Festivals of Laughter' from the campaign for freedom of expression organized in January 1994 by the South African National Arts Coalition (NAC), one year after the Munich event. Theoretically anchored in the Bakhtinian carnival tradition of 'denuding, unmasking and uprooting power structures' (II, p. 29) in literature, she examines the way in which the linguistic domination of English has been 'carnivalised' (II, p. 33) in writing and the performing arts in post-apartheid South Africa. In that respect, the dub poet and 'doctor of rap' Lesogo Rampolokeng is, all by himself, a dancing monument to the South African polyglossic situation. He speaks 'English and the Johannesburg slang, a mix of mainly Xhosa, Zulu, Afrikaans and English' (II, p. 32). although Veit-Wild cautions that 'in Zimbabwe, syncretic literary forms as expressions of a hybrid consciousness are less developed than in South Africa' (II, p. 34), the forums for the Zimbabwe women writers, a grass-roots organization founded in 1990, are in themselves 'birthplaces of syncretism'. In contrast the Bulawayo-based Amakhosi Theatre draws on 'traditional dance and song as well as on modern urban culture, using "Ndenglish", a mélange of English and street Ndebele' (II, p. 35), a mixture that remains quite sedate if gauged against Dambudzo Marechera's irreverent but most idiosyncratic pronouncement: 'In Zimbabwe we have these two great indigenous languages, Chishona and Sindebele . . . Who wants us to keep writing these shit-Shona and shit-Ndebele languages, this missionary chickenshit? Who else but the imperialists?' (II, p. 36). The pressures of language are such that no language policy can hold within its bounds the monstrous buoyancy of language behaviour in Africa.

### 3. 'Can you cook books and feed them to your husband?': The predicament of gender

This is what a father says to his daughter in Tsitsi Dangarembga's *Nervous Conditions*, the first novel in English by a black Zimbabwean woman. This shows that, rather than culture, woman is in a predicament of the most inextricable kind. Viera Pawlikowa-Vilhanowa from Bratislava and the Cameroonian scholar Nalova Lyonga take in their purview such writers as Flora Nwapa, Ama Ata Aidoo, Rebeka Njau, Bessie Head, Werewere Liking, Mariama Bâ and the indomitable Tsitsi. Despite the growing interest in gender and women's studies, they both note that male writers continue to 'invariably define ideal womanhood in terms of motherhood' (I, p. 170) and that 'African literary studies were and continue to be an almost masculine domain' (I, p. 173). As African women writers are looking for 'a hoe of one's own', after Virginia Woolf's 'A Room of One's Own', they are still aiming to develop an indigenous brand of feminism that need not lead to embracing, as Flora Nwapa did, Alice Walker's 'womanism'. (I. p. 162). The two scholars agree that the female critic has a responsibility to correct 'false images of women in Africa' (I, p. 175), and possibly to extend that responsibility to Molara Ogundipe-Leslie's three degrees of commitment – as a writer, as a woman, and as a third world person. This commitment, however, should not exclude a sisterhood between Western and non-Western. As a result Showalter's anthology *The New Feminist Criticism* (1986) is seen as a sisterly 'companion volume' to Carol Boyce Davies' *Ngambika*. Despite the good will behind both articles, they fail to link the feminist import with the 'alternative forms of expression', which was the conference theme – unless one understands 'alternative' as a substitute for 'feminine'! In that respect, the two articles under 'Gender and Postcolonialism' in the second volume are more energetic and more to the point, possibly because they both deal with *Nervous Conditions*, a phrase originally applied by Frantz Fanon in his *Wretched of the Earth* (1961) to colonized peoples. The female body is at the centre of Heike Härting's preoccupations, as it is still a crucial site of male ideological struggle as well as a site of difference. Dangaremgba's novel and Margaret Atwood's *The Edible Woman* are re-read as 'medical histories of colonialism' that highlight frequently marginalized psychological effects 'such as schizophrenia, anorexia nervosa, or heteronomy generally' (II, p. 237). Härting gives the lie to Lilli Gast's *Magersucht* (1989) which considers anorexia as 'exclusively a feature of Western individual societies' (II, p. 239) by presenting it as 'a fertile metaphor in postcolonial and feminist discourse' (II, p. 244) and, more largely, by rewriting history 'through the reappropriation of the female body as erogenous reading-and writing-space' (II, p. 245).

If 'I' is for some anorexic writers the slenderest pronoun in the English language, 'we' is to 'wo(e)men' the most festive and communal pronoun. That Carola Torti, Karin Kilb and the token-male of this troika, Mark Stein, got together to 'grope for coherence' is definitely a sign of the times. Although these articles on women prove that the subaltern cannot speak because 'representation' has not yet withered away, they also serve as reminders that, as Spivak concludes in her seminal article, 'there is no virtue in global laundry lists with "woman" as a pious term.'[4] Syncretism as a producer of hyphenated identities should do well to encompass gendered identities, as well, for the new idioms to emerge in the next century will have to be roomy and ample enough to accommodate androgyny in a post-cultural era.

Université catholique de Louvain, Louvain-la-Neuve, Belgium

## NOTES

1. Bayreuth African Series, 1994, 216 pp. ISBN 3-927510-31-9.
2. See, for instance, Rita Felsky, 'On Confession,' *Beyond Feminist Aesthetics* (London: Hutchinson Radiu, 1989).
3. Leigh Gilmore, *Autobiographics: A Feminist Theory of Women's Self-Representation* (Ithaca: Cornell University Press, 1994).
4. Gayatri Chakravorty Spivak, 'Can the Subaltern Speak?,' in *Marxism and the Interpretation of Culture*, eds. C. Nelson & L. Grossberg (Basingstoke: Macmillan Education, 1988), 313 pp.

---

Régis Fanchette. *A Private Journey . . . itinéraire privé*. Editions de l'Océan Indien, 1996, 127 pp.
Distributed by African Books Collective, 27 Park End Street, Oxford OX1 1HU

Introduced by the author as a 'quasi anthology' this book of an altogether uncommon kind consists of some 50 pieces selected by Fanchette himself. They include short fiction, memoirs, criticism, poems and even a short extract from a play. The selection is bilingual English – French, not, as one might expect, because pieces are offered with their translations, but because Fanchette writes in both French (his mother tongue) and in English (an acquired language he perfectly masters).[1] Now retired, Régis Fanchette is a Mauritian teacher of English who became General Manager of the Mauritius Government Tourist Office. There is great appeal in his commitment to the written word, in his determination to put his island – Mauritius – on the literary map in both English and French, and in the outgoing enthusiasm that infuses his texts. There may be some naïveté in his plea for the English language in that English is probably the language in the world that least needs defending.

It is somewhat aggravating to notice the discrepancy between on the one hand the belief he voices in his introduction that a language must be free to expand and roam instead of being held in check and on the other the classical overcorrectness with which he uses both English and French. His prose pieces particularly often read like prize-winning school essays, with exactly the right number of predictable comparisons, adjectives and metaphors, with the expected touch of humour and the convincing personal note. The dramatic extract he includes belongs to a heavily literary (somewhat overwritten) form of theatre, closer to Claudel and Eliot, say, than to Wesker or Obaldia, or, for that matter, Pinter or Ionesco. Characters stand in front of each other pompously displaying their hearts on their sleeves and declaiming elevated feelings, with no attempt at either realistic mimicry or Brechtian Gestus. The complete absence of an ear for dialogue and for real speech is perceptible in his short stories too. His characters speak 'as they do in books', which may be intentional, but I suspect is not. In fact his literary models are such now canonical and canonized writers as Baudelaire and Keats.

Some of his poems are less stilted. His lightly tripping 'Rondeau', for instance, takes off quite nicely. The dialogue in 'Contretemps et contrepoint' is pregnant with a moving intensity:

Voyageur et passeur, rentre chez toi.
Ces nuages décrochés ne sont qu'orties
aux lambeaux de ta chair; .
que débris de ton coeur.

Other poems lack any sense of a shaping rhythm, though they offer some lively descriptions:

and then I turn with some relief
to the muddy-coated Creole bitch
your despised house mate
with its tail like a bamboo broom
sweeping all on its way
and abundant of motion
falling over the whole place
as over people
her yet endearing manners
still unworthy of your disdainful airs. (To my whippet)

In some cases they waver between maudlin clichés and genuine finds, as in 'Marine sur Seine' ('Sur une île balisée hors le temps et l'espace, gibbeuse et nimbée de son seul devenir'). Deprived though we may feel of some literary daring and creativeness, we should acknowledge that this kind of polished writing is typical of writers who feel that they have to match metropolitan models and, however unconsciously, comply with classical literary recipes. Without them, the next generation might not have felt free to develop their own literature. In this sense, Régis Fanchette belongs to the trailblazers.

Christine Pagnoulle
University of Liège, Belgium

## NOTES

1. One could even argue that the collection is trilingual since one of the poems – 'Contretemps et contrepoint', with its homage to Jacques Brel, Cervantes, Machado, and the man of La Mancha – is accompanied by a Spanish translation.

# Index

145